PMA SCIENCE STOIC

WISDOM TO CONQUER THE DAY

JAY PACHECO

CONTENTS

PMA Science Stoic
Wisdom to Conquer the Day
Copyright © 2024 PMA© Science LLC
All rights reserved.

ISBN **978 82 94011 35 3** eBook
ISBN **978 82 94011 34 6** Softcover USA
ISBN **978-82-94011-41-4** Softcover UK
ISBN Audiobook

Copyright Note

DISCLAIMER
The material in this book is provided for educational and informational purposes only. The author takes no responsibility for any results or outcomes from using this material.

Design of the book cover by Maham Khan

JAY PACHECO'S BOOKS

Akhbi-Yahwa: JHVH Protects
The Magic of Gratitude
Aztec - Mexican
PMA Science of Psychology
The Stoic Journey
The Stoic Mindset Planner
PMA Science of Habit
PMA Science: The Short Stories of Luna
Diorama: Short Collections of Poems

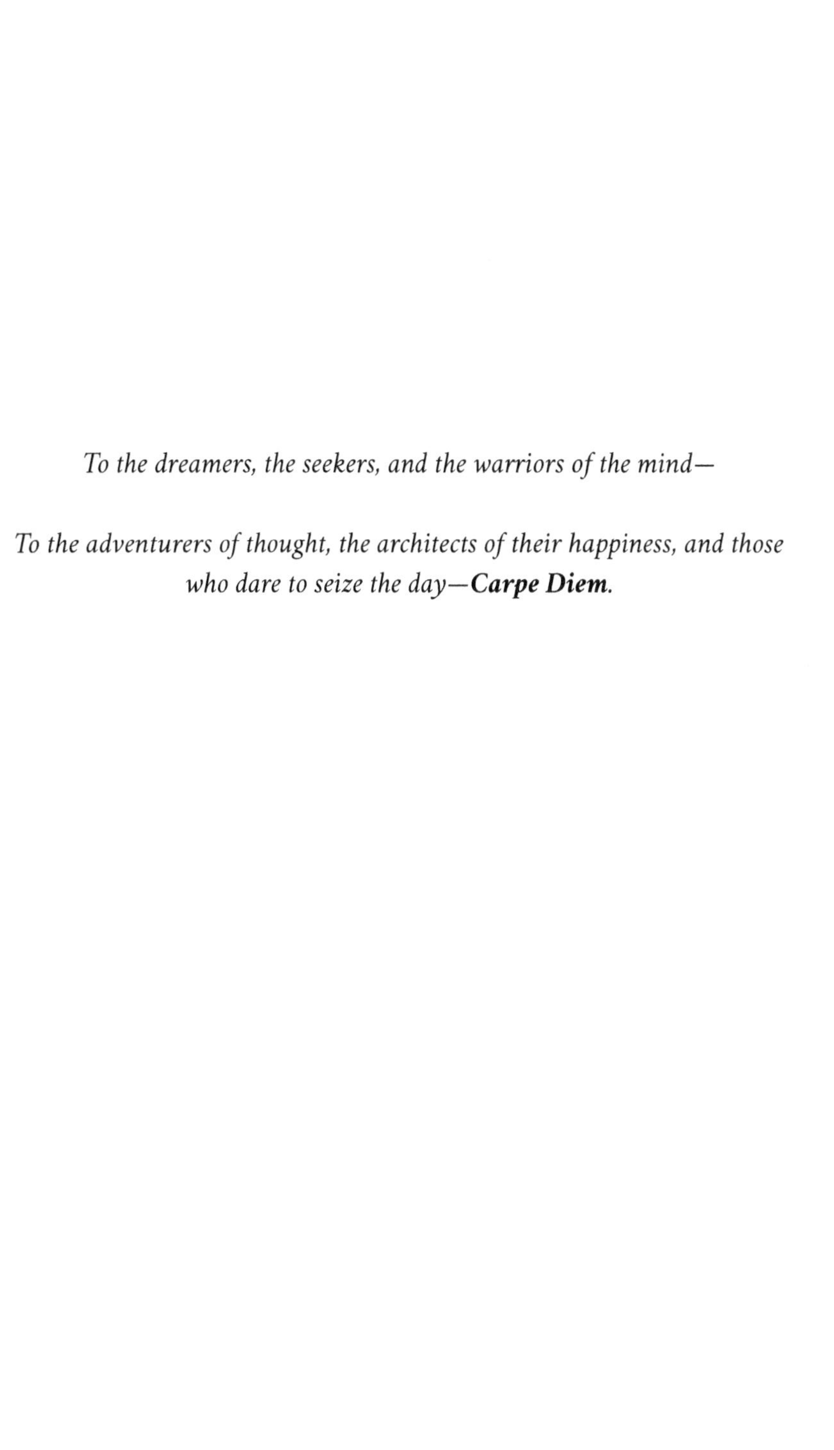

To the dreamers, the seekers, and the warriors of the mind—

*To the adventurers of thought, the architects of their happiness, and those who dare to seize the day—**Carpe Diem**.*

CARPE DIEM

You are about to begin one of the most exciting chapters of your life, and you will love it.

Carpe Diem: "seize the day."

The Origin of *Carpe Diem*

This Latin phrase, which means "pluck the day," was used by the Roman poet Horace to express the idea that we should enjoy life while we can. His full injunction, "carpe diem quam minimum credula postero," can be translated as "pluck the day, trusting as little as possible in the next one," but *carpe diem* alone has come to be used as shorthand for this entire idea, which is more widely known as "seize the day."

HOW THIS GUIDE IS STRUCTURED

This guide serves as your compass for mastering each day with wisdom, clarity, and resilience. Drawing from the timeless teachings of Stoicism, a touch of Positive Mental Attitude (PMA), and modern psychology, it provides practical strategies to help you navigate life's challenges with grace and effectiveness.

Inside, you'll discover actionable Stoic principles and rules designed to empower your mindset, foster emotional balance, and enhance your daily habits. Along with these insights, we've included valuable resources and links to deepen your understanding and support your personal growth.

Thank you for subscribing to our newsletter and embarking on this transformative journey. May these pages serve as a toolkit to help you seize every day with purpose and intention.

The adventure begins—Carpe Diem!

PREFACE

In a world that spins faster than ever, where the relentless flow of information blurs the line between urgency and chaos, where pressures mount, and expectations never relent, wisdom, clarity, and calm have become the most precious companions. How do we navigate this labyrinth of modern life without losing ourselves? How do we find steadiness amidst the storm? This is where the timeless philosophy of Stoicism steps in—not as an escape, but as a powerful guide.

Born over two thousand years ago in the heart of ancient Greece and Rome, Stoicism emerged as a philosophy for life, grounded in the simple yet profound understanding that existence is beautiful and brutal. Its teachings, forged by the sharp minds of thinkers like Epictetus, Seneca, and Marcus Aurelius, are not relics to be admired from a distance but living, breathing wisdom that illuminates the path to resilience, clarity, and inner peace.

This book, *"Stoic Wisdom to Conquer the Day,"* is not a dusty historical exploration nor a detached academic study. Instead, it is a bridge—connecting ancient truths with modern challenges, a compass for navigating the uncharted waters of daily life. Consider this an invitation to embark on a transformative journey that challenges, inspires, and equips you to lead a life of balance, courage, and purpose.

Through these pages, you will encounter the teachings of the Stoics and their living applications. You will find engaging stories, vivid illustrations, and practical tools that make Stoicism accessible to all. These lessons are not lofty ideals—they are meant for the real world, for the struggles and triumphs that define our humanity. Whether you're grappling with the pressures of a demanding career, navigating the complexities of relationships, or simply striving to find peace amidst the noise, Stoicism offers profound insights that speak to the heart of these challenges.

Some may wonder how a philosophy from ancient times could resonate in today's hyper-connected, fast-paced reality. The answer lies in a simple truth: while the world around us has transformed, the essence of the human experience has not. We still wrestle with uncertainty, loss, frustration, and the search for meaning. Stoicism doesn't pretend to solve these mysteries—it teaches us how to face them with grace, strength, and wisdom.

Marcus Aurelius once wrote, *"You have power over your mind—not outside events. Realize this, and you will find strength."* This is the promise of Stoicism: not the elimination of adversity but the empowerment to rise above it. By embracing these principles, you will learn to find calm in the chaos, courage in the face of fear, and joy even in the simplest moments.

As you turn these pages, you will uncover timeless lessons wrapped in inspiring anecdotes and practical steps. You will walk alongside the great Stoics and see their wisdom come alive in today's world. But more importantly, you will discover how this wisdom can illuminate your path, making you more centered, reflective, and empowered.

This book is not the final destination—it's the beginning of a journey —a journey into yourself, the depths of your potential, and the timeless truths that have guided countless seekers before you. As you explore Stoicism's teachings, I hope you will uncover its historical richness and transformative power to reshape your life today.

Welcome to the wisdom that has transcended centuries. Welcome to a philosophy that promises understanding, fulfillment, and the strength to face whatever challenges lie ahead. Let us walk these ancient paths together and discover the enduring truths that make us stronger, wiser, and more human.

Let the journey begin.

PART I

Stoic Wisdom to Conquer the Day

UNDERSTANDING STOICISM

The Philosophy of Control

"We suffer more often in imagination than in reality." - Seneca

IN A WORLD that moves at breakneck speed—where uncertainties lurk around every corner, and pressures mount relentlessly—finding a sense of control can feel like grasping at smoke. Yet, amidst the chaos, Stoicism offers a profound, empowering truth: clarity emerges when we distinguish between what we can control and cannot. This simple philosophy transforms our relationship with life, guiding us to contentment, purpose, and resilience.

AS MARCUS AURELIUS WISELY NOTED, *"You have power over your mind—not outside events. Realize this, and you will find strength."* This is the essence of Stoicism, a philosophy that elegantly marries simplicity with depth. It invites us to focus on the present, embrace life's uncertainties, and channel our energy toward what truly matters. Through this lens, we learn to survive and thrive within life's unpredictabilities.

WHAT IS STOICISM?

AT ITS CORE, Stoicism is a way of life that emphasizes emotional mastery, self-control, and harmony with nature. The philosophy traces its origins to ancient Greece, where Zeno of Citium, the founder, taught in a humble *stoa*—a covered porch open to all. From this unassuming beginning emerged a profound system of thought that resonates today.

THE WORD *STOA* reflects Stoicism's spirit: an open, safe space for intellectual exploration and growth. Zeno chose the porch not out of necessity alone but as a symbol of accessibility and inclusion. His teachings were not confined to the elite but to anyone seeking wisdom, resilience, and inner peace.

THE STOICS TAUGHT that a good life is achieved not by controlling external events but by mastering our internal world. They emphasized virtues like wisdom, courage, justice, and temperance and advocated a life aligned with reason and nature. Their teachings remain a mental and emotional well-being cornerstone, offering timeless guidance for modern challenges.

THE DICHOTOMY of Control

. . .

CENTRAL TO STOICISM is the *Dichotomy of Control*—the distinction between what we can and cannot influence. This principle is both liberating and empowering. By recognizing that some things are beyond our control, we free ourselves from unnecessary worry and focus our efforts on what we can change.

EXAMPLE 1: The Garden of Life

IMAGINE a garden blooming with vibrant flowers and invasive weeds. You can nurture the flowers carefully and remove the weeds, but you cannot control the weather. In life, we can focus on our actions—our efforts, decisions, and attitudes—while accepting the unpredictability of external circumstances. This balance of action and acceptance fosters growth and fulfillment.

EXAMPLE 2: Navigating Your Career

THE ECONOMY or company decisions may be beyond your control in your career. However, your work ethic, skills, and attitude are within your influence. By focusing on these, you increase your chances of success and cultivate a sense of personal mastery and empowerment. As Epictetus said, *"It's not what happens to you, but how you react to it that matters."*

ACCEPTANCE: A Path to Peace

MUCH OF OUR anxiety stems from resisting reality. We fret over traffic jams, missed opportunities, or unforeseen challenges—all outside our control. Stoicism teaches us to accept life as it unfolds and to find peace in the present moment.

EXAMPLE: The Traffic Jam

PICTURE YOURSELF STUCK IN A GRIDLOCK, late for an important meeting. While frustration may seem inevitable, a Stoic mindset offers an alternative. Instead of fixating on the immovable traffic, you could use the time to prepare mentally for the meeting or reflect on your goals. As Seneca reminds us, *"We suffer more often in imagination than in reality."*

THE POWER of Perspective

STOICISM IS NOT ABOUT passive resignation but about reframing challenges as growth opportunities. We can reclaim our power and find freedom by shifting our focus from external obstacles to internal strengths.

EXAMPLE: A Challenging Project

MANY MIGHT FIND a daunting project at work overwhelming, but a Stoic sees it differently. Instead of succumbing to stress, they view the challenge as a chance to grow, learn, and demonstrate resilience. This perspective transforms obstacles into stepping stones, fostering personal and professional growth.

APPLYING Stoicism in Daily Life

· · ·

THE BEAUTY of Stoicism lies in its practicality. It offers tools for navigating life's complexities with grace and intention. By mastering our emotions and focusing on what we can control, we cultivate a life of purpose and mindfulness.

EXAMPLE 1: Managing Relationships

IF A FRIEND REACTS HARSHLY to your opinion, your instinct might be to feel hurt or defensive. Stoicism, however, teaches you to recognize that their reaction is outside your control. What you *can* control is your response—choosing empathy and composure over anger. This approach not only preserves the relationship but also strengthens your emotional resilience.

EXAMPLE 2: Facing Health Challenges

WHEN CONFRONTED WITH A HEALTH ISSUE, a Stoic focuses on actionable steps like maintaining a healthy diet, exercising, and fostering a positive mindset. Rather than lamenting the situation, they channel their energy into what they can control, creating a sense of agency and hope.

THE FREEDOM in Understanding Control

BY EMBRACING the Stoic principle of control, we unburden ourselves from unnecessary anxieties. This clarity allows us to focus on what truly matters—our growth, relationships, and contributions to the world. We discover a profound sense of freedom and peace as we let go of what we cannot change.

Closing Thoughts: Stoicism in Practice

THE WISDOM of Stoicism is not confined to ancient texts or lofty ideals —it is a living philosophy, relevant and transformative. As you internalize its principles, you will be equipped to face life's challenges with courage and composure.

To QUOTE Marcus Aurelius once more: *"The happiness of your life depends upon the quality of your thoughts."* By focusing on what you can control and letting go of the rest, you open the door to a life of tranquility, purpose, and mastery.

LET Stoicism be your compass in the ever-changing landscape of life. Its teachings are not just a philosophy—they are a way of living, a guide to thriving amidst the chaos. As we continue this journey together, may you find the wisdom, strength, and serenity that Stoicism offers.

STOIC DISCIPLINES

The Art of Virtuous Living

IN AN ERA BRIMMING with distractions and complexity, the timeless wisdom of Stoicism calls us to return to simplicity and purpose. At its heart, Stoicism is a philosophy of action, reflection, and alignment—a practical guide to living virtuously in harmony with nature and reason. The Oxford Dictionary explains that Stoicism teaches *"self-control and virtuous living in alignment with nature."* But what does this look like in practice?

IN THIS CHAPTER, we move beyond definitions and delve into Stoicism's three foundational disciplines: the Discipline of Desire, the Discipline of Action, and the Discipline of Assent. These disciplines form the backbone of Stoic practice and empower us to navigate life's uncertainties with clarity, resilience, and grace.

. . .

THE THREE DISCIPLINES of Stoicism

THE STOICS UNDERSTOOD that the best way to approach life's challenges is to cultivate mastery over three key areas: our desires, actions, and judgments. Let's explore each discipline in detail and uncover how it can transform how we live, think, and interact with the world.

1. The Discipline of Desire (Or Will)

"He who has learned to desire only what is in his power has learned the secret of contentment." — Epictetus

THE DISCIPLINE OF DESIRE teaches us to align our wants with what is within our control. It encourages us to release attachment to external outcomes and focus instead on our efforts and intentions. This discipline is not about suppressing desire but refining it—channeling our energy toward what we can influence and letting go of what lies beyond our grasp.

EXAMPLE: The Farmer and the Weather

IMAGINE a farmer planting seeds in his field. He carefully prepares the soil, waters the crops, and protects them from pests. These actions are within his control. However, the weather—a crucial factor in the harvest—remains beyond his influence. Stoicism teaches the farmer to focus on his diligent efforts and accept the outcomes, whatever they may be. By embracing this mindset, the farmer finds peace, knowing he has done his part.

. . .

IN LIFE, we are all like this farmer. Whether pursuing career goals, nurturing relationships, or striving for personal growth, we can only control our actions—not the results. The Discipline of Desire frees us from unnecessary anxiety and empowers us to act with integrity and intention.

2. The Discipline of Action (Or Duty)

"Waste no more time arguing about what a good man should be. Be one." — Marcus Aurelius

THE DISCIPLINE OF ACTION centers on how we live, work, and interact with others. It calls us to act virtuously, fulfilling our societal roles with integrity, courage, and kindness. Stoicism teaches that our actions should align with our values and the greater good, regardless of external recognition or reward.

EXAMPLE: The Dedicated Teacher

CONSIDER a teacher passionately committed to her students' growth. She pours her energy into crafting engaging lessons, offering guidance, and encouraging curiosity. Her dedication reflects her understanding of her role as an educator. Even if her efforts go unrecognized, she remains steadfast, knowing that her actions align with her purpose.

. . .

THIS DISCIPLINE REMINDS us that virtue lies in the doing, not the outcome. By fulfilling our responsibilities sincerely and excellently, we contribute to a harmonious society and find meaning in our endeavors.

3. The Discipline of Assent (Or Judgment)

"The chief task in life is simply this: to identify and separate matters so that I can say clearly to myself which are externals not under my control and which have to do with the choices I actually control." — Epictetus

THE DISCIPLINE OF ASSENT is evaluating our thoughts, perceptions, and judgments. It challenges us to see things as they are—not as we wish or fear them. This discipline cultivates mindfulness and objectivity, helping us respond to situations with wisdom rather than emotion.

EXAMPLE: The Traffic Jam

PICTURE YOURSELF STUCK in a traffic jam, late for an important meeting. Frustration bubbles up as you glance at the clock. A Stoic, however, would pause and recognize that traffic is beyond their control. Instead of stewing in anger, they might use the time to prepare for the meeting or reflect on their goals mentally. They regain clarity and composure by assenting only to what is true—"I am in traffic, and it is out of my control."

. . .

THIS DISCIPLINE IS a powerful tool for navigating life's challenges. It teaches us to question our assumptions, release unhelpful narratives, and make decisions rooted in reality rather than reaction.

The Harmony of the Three Disciplines

THE THREE DISCIPLINES of Stoicism are not isolated practices—they interweave to create a holistic approach to life. Together, they offer a roadmap for virtuous living:

• **THE DISCIPLINE of Desire** guides us to focus on what we can control, fostering serenity and resilience.

• **THE DISCIPLINE OF ACTION** inspires us to act purposefully, contributing to the greater good.

• **THE DISCIPLINE OF ASSENT** sharpens our perception, helping us see the world clearly and truthfully.

THESE DISCIPLINES EMPOWER us to face life's complexities with grace, wisdom, and courage when applied together.

Practical Applications of Stoic Disciplines

STOICISM IS NOT a philosophy confined to ancient texts or theoretical musings—it is a living, breathing practice meant to be applied daily.

Here are some examples of how the Stoic disciplines can be integrated into modern scenarios:

EXAMPLE 1: Navigating Relationships

IF A FRIEND REBUKES YOU, your initial reaction might be defensiveness or hurt. The Discipline of Assent reminds you to separate their words from your worth, recognizing that their reaction may stem from their struggles. The Discipline of Action then calls you to respond with empathy and patience, maintaining the integrity of the relationship.

EXAMPLE 2: Overcoming Setbacks

IMAGINE FACING A PROFESSIONAL FAILURE, such as a rejected proposal or missed promotion. The Discipline of Desire helps you accept the outcome without self-reproach, focusing instead on refining your skills. The Discipline of Action motivates you to persevere, while the Discipline of Assent enables you to see the setback as a learning opportunity rather than a defeat.

A PATH to Freedom and Fulfillment

THE STOIC DISCIPLINES offer more than just guidance—they offer freedom. By aligning our desires, actions, and judgments with what is within our control, we free ourselves from the shackles of frustration, fear, and regret. Seneca observed, *"A happy life is one which is in accordance with its own nature."*

· · ·

THROUGH THESE DISCIPLINES, we discover the art of virtuous living—a way of life that nurtures tranquility, purpose, and resilience. Stoicism provides a framework for navigating life's challenges with wisdom and grace, no matter your role or circumstance. Its principles are as relevant today as in ancient times, serving as a beacon of light for those seeking to live well.

AS WE MOVE FORWARD, remember that Stoicism is not about perfection but progress. Each day offers an opportunity to practice these disciplines, refining your character and deepening your understanding. With patience and perseverance, the path of Stoicism will lead you to a life of meaning, mastery, and fulfillment.

LET us walk this path together, embracing the wisdom of the Stoics as a guide to our virtuous journey.

THE FOUR CARDINAL VIRTUES

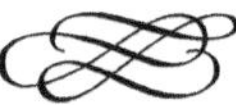

$\mathcal{S}$ toic Disciplines: The Four Cardinal Virtues

THE COMPASS of Stoic Ethics

IN THE WHIRLWIND of modern life, where choices overwhelm, and challenges loom large, we often search for a steadying force—a compass to guide us. Stoicism, with its timeless wisdom, provides just that. At its heart lie the Four Cardinal Virtues: **Wisdom**, **Courage**, **Justice**, and **Temperance**. These virtues are not mere philosophical ideals but practical, actionable principles that empower us to live with purpose, integrity, and balance. They teach us to cultivate inner strength, nurture meaningful relationships, and find peace amid chaos.

As MARCUS AURELIUS WROTE, *"If it is not right, do not do it; if it is not true, do not say it."* This succinctly encapsulates the Stoic ethos—a life guided by virtue and reason. Let us explore these virtues not as abstract concepts but as living tools that can transform how we think, act, and interact with the world.

WISDOM: **The Guiding Light**

"Knowing yourself is the beginning of all wisdom." — Aristotle

WISDOM IS MORE than intellectual knowledge; it is the ability to see the world as it truly is and respond with clarity and understanding. It allows us to discern what matters and does not, empowering us to make decisions rooted in truth and reason. Wisdom is not static; it grows through experience, reflection, and learning.

EXAMPLE: **The Workplace Challenge**

IMAGINE you're faced with a complex problem at work. Instead of reacting impulsively, a Stoic would pause, gather facts, seek advice from trusted colleagues, and carefully consider the consequences before acting. Wisdom helps us recognize our limitations, remain open to learning, and focus on what we can control.

EXAMPLE: **The Lesson of Pain**

REMEMBER the first time you touched a hot stove as a child? The pain taught you a lasting lesson: avoid what harms you. This simple yet profound experience reflects the essence of wisdom—learning from life's challenges and using those lessons to guide future actions. Wisdom transforms pain into growth and mistakes into mastery.

COURAGE: **The Heart of Stoicism**

"Courage is not the absence of fear but the triumph over it." — Nelson Mandela

COURAGE IN STOICISM encompasses not only physical bravery but also the moral strength to do what is right, even when facing adversity. It demands resilience, determination, and the willingness to act with integrity despite fear, uncertainty, or opposition.

EXAMPLE: **Standing Up for Justice**

IMAGINE you witness a colleague engaging in unethical behavior. It would be easier to stay silent, avoiding conflict. However, a Stoic, grounded in courage, would confront the situation or report the behavior, knowing that integrity sometimes demands uncomfortable choices. Courage is the backbone of moral action, enabling us to uphold our principles despite the high cost.

COURAGE REMINDS us that our obstacles are not barriers but opportunities to grow stronger. As Seneca said, *"Difficulties strengthen the mind, as labor does the body."*

JUSTICE: **The Foundation of Fairness**

"Justice is the constant and perpetual will to render to each his due." — Ulpian

JUSTICE IN STOICISM is about treating others with fairness, dignity, and respect. It extends beyond legal definitions to encompass our moral obligations to others. Justice calls us to recognize every individual's intrinsic value and act in ways that promote equity and harmony.

EXAMPLE: **The Fair Leader**

IMAGINE you're a manager tasked with distributing bonuses. A Stoic leader would base these decisions on merit and performance, avoiding favoritism or bias. Justice ensures that everyone is treated fairly and respectfully, fostering trust and unity in the workplace.

JUSTICE ALSO APPLIES to how we treat ourselves. Self-compassion is a form of justice, reminding us to honor our worth and care for our well-being without self-criticism or neglect.

TEMPERANCE: **The Art of Balance**

"Nothing in excess, everything in moderation." — Delphic Maxim

TEMPERANCE IS the virtue of self-control and moderation. It is the ability to resist excess, maintain balance, and align our actions with our values. Temperance helps us avoid the extremes of indulgence and deprivation, fostering a life of harmony and fulfillment.

EXAMPLE: Financial Prudence

CONSIDER MANAGING YOUR FINANCES. Temperance would guide you to spend within your means, save for the future, and avoid unnecessary extravagance. This balance ensures financial stability and aligns your spending habits with long-term goals and values.

EXAMPLE: Emotional Self-Control

IMAGINE you're provoked during a heated argument. Temperance would encourage you to pause, take a deep breath, and respond thoughtfully rather than lashing out in anger. By mastering your emotions, you defuse tension and preserve the integrity of the relationship.

INTEGRATING the Virtues in Daily Life

THE FOUR CARDINAL Virtues are not standalone principles—they work harmoniously, weaving a tapestry of virtuous living. Together, they guide us toward making wise decisions, acting courageously, treating others fairly, and maintaining balance in all aspects of life.

EXAMPLE: Facing Career Challenges

. . .

IMAGINE you're in a job where your contributions go unnoticed.

• **Wisdom** helps you evaluate the situation objectively, understanding what is within your control.

• **Courage** empowers you to voice your ideas and seek growth opportunities, even if it feels uncomfortable.

• **Justice** ensures your decisions honor your responsibilities to yourself and others.

• **Temperance** helps you maintain emotional balance, focusing on long-term goals rather than immediate frustrations.

BY APPLYING THESE VIRTUES, you not only navigate challenges but also grow stronger, wiser, and more resilient.

LIVING THE VIRTUES: A Path to Fulfillment

THE FOUR CARDINAL Virtues are more than ethical ideals; they are practical tools for navigating life's complexities with integrity and purpose. They encourage us to:

• *Think profoundly and act wisely (Wisdom).*
• *Face challenges with courage and confidence (Courage).*
• *Treat others with fairness and respect (Justice).*
• *Live with balance and self-control (Temperance).*

INTEGRATING these virtues into our lives cultivates a more profound sense of meaning, connection, and fulfillment.

IN A WORLD often marked by confusion and moral ambiguity, these virtues serve as an unwavering compass, guiding us to act with clarity and conviction. They remind us that a virtuous life is not about perfection but progress—a continuous journey toward becoming the best version of ourselves.

AS EPICTETUS WROTE, *"First say to yourself what you would be; and then do what you have to do."* The Four Cardinal Virtues offer a blueprint for this transformation, helping us align our actions with our highest aspirations.

LET us embrace these virtues not as distant ideals but as daily practices. With Stoicism as our guide, we can live lives of courage, wisdom, justice, and balance, creating a legacy of integrity and purpose for ourselves and those around us.

STOICISM IN ACTION

*P*ractical Pathways to Everyday Resilience

STOICISM ISN'T CONFINED to ancient philosophy or lofty intellectual debate; its true power emerges daily. It thrives in the ordinary, offering tools to cultivate resilience, contentment, and virtue through intentional action. It's a practical philosophy that transforms thought into action, enabling us to navigate challenges, embrace growth, and find meaning in the seemingly mundane.

THIS CHAPTER EXPLORES how Stoicism becomes a lived practice—a framework for addressing life's complexities with grace and purpose. With its insights, we can untangle the psychological biases and emotional habits that lead to distress. We can create a fulfilling, harmonious life by cultivating gratitude, focusing on what's within our control, and living with intention. As Marcus Aurelius said, *"You have power over your mind—not outside events. Realize this, and you will find strength."*

. . .

STARTING the Day with the Intention

"The soul becomes dyed with the color of its thoughts." — Marcus Aurelius

THE STOICS BELIEVED in beginning each day with mindfulness, setting the tone for purposeful living. By reflecting on what lies ahead, we can mentally prepare for challenges, embrace opportunities, and focus on what truly matters. This practice is not about anticipating perfection but building resilience for the inevitable ups and downs of the day.

EXAMPLE: The Teacher's Challenge

IMAGINE a teacher preparing for a challenging class. Instead of dreading potential disruptions, they begin the day reflecting on the virtues of patience, empathy, and diligence. This mindset equips them to face the class with grace and composure, focusing on creating a positive learning environment. This intention-setting fosters a productive atmosphere and helps prevent burnout, allowing teachers to find joy in their work despite the challenges.

FACING Challenges with Composure

"We suffer more often in imagination than in reality." — Seneca

LIFE IS RIFE WITH OBSTACLES, but Stoicism teaches us to face them calmly and clearly. We can overcome challenges without succumbing to panic or frustration by mastering our emotions and focusing on constructive action. Stoic resilience lies in accepting setbacks as part of life and responding to them with thoughtful determination.

EXAMPLE: The Unexpected Work Setback

IMAGINE your work project encounters an unforeseen hurdle. A Stoic approach involves pausing to assess the situation, breaking the problem into manageable steps, and addressing each with focus. Instead of wasting energy on blame or worry, you channel your efforts into finding solutions. This practical mindset resolves the issue and strengthens your problem-solving skills for future challenges.

EMBRACING Adversity as Opportunity

"What stands in the way becomes the way." — Marcus Aurelius

STOICISM REFRAMES ADVERSITY as an opportunity for growth. No matter how daunting, challenges are invitations to strengthen our character, refine our skills, and deepen our understanding of life. By embracing this perspective, we transform setbacks into stepping stones.

EXAMPLE: The Athlete's Loss

. . .

PICTURE AN ATHLETE who loses a critical match. Instead of despairing, they use the experience to identify weaknesses, refine techniques, and build mental toughness. A Stoic mindset views failure not as a defeat but a lesson—a catalyst for improvement. As Epictetus reminds us, *"Difficulties show what men are."*

BUILDING Relationships through Empathy and Respect

"Be tolerant with others and strict with yourself." — Marcus Aurelius

HUMAN RELATIONSHIPS ARE central to a fulfilling life, and Stoicism emphasizes treating others with kindness, empathy, and respect. Understanding different perspectives and prioritizing fairness strengthen our connections and foster harmony.

EXAMPLE: Navigating a Difficult Colleague

DEALING with a challenging coworker can be frustrating. A Stoic approaches the situation empathetically, seeking to understand their perspective and finding common ground. This mindset transforms potential conflict into collaboration, cultivating mutual respect and a healthier work environment. Stoicism teaches us that our reactions—not others' actions—determine the quality of our relationships.

ENDING the Day with Reflection

"What is not good for the swarm is not good for the bee." — Marcus Aurelius

Reflection is a cornerstone of Stoic practice. Reviewing the day's events, we identify successes, learn from missteps, and prepare for tomorrow. This habit fosters continuous growth, encouraging us to refine our actions and align them with our values.

EXAMPLE: The Evening Reflection

AT THE END of a busy day, you take a few minutes to reflect: What went well? Where did you stumble? What lessons can you carry forward? This simple practice transforms daily experiences into opportunities for growth, cultivating a sense of gratitude and purpose. Seneca noted, *"As is a tale, so is life: not how long it is, but how good it is, is what matters."*

PRACTICAL TOOLS for Living Stoicism

1 Morning Reflection: Begin your day by setting intentions. Reflect on the challenges ahead and the virtues you wish to embody, such as patience, courage, or gratitude.

2 Dichotomy of Control: Separate what is within your control (your thoughts and actions) from what is not (others' opinions, external events). Focus your energy where it matters.

3 Pause and Reframe: When faced with adversity, pause and reframe the challenge as an opportunity to learn, adapt, or grow.

4 Daily Gratitude: Acknowledge the positives in your life, no matter how small. Gratitude fosters resilience and contentment.

5 Evening Reflection: End your day by reviewing your actions, learning from missteps, and appreciating your progress.

STOICISM AS A WAY of Life

"First say to yourself what you would be, and then do what you have to do."
— Epictetus

STOICISM IS MORE THAN A PHILOSOPHY—IT's a way of life. It invites us to actively engage with our experiences, embracing each day with intention, courage, and wisdom. Whether you're a student tackling exams, a parent managing responsibilities, or a professional navigating challenges, Stoicism offers practical tools to thrive.

BY INTEGRATING Stoic principles into daily practices, you cultivate a life rich in purpose and resilience. You learn to find joy in the journey, embrace growth through adversity, and build meaningful relationships. In the chaotic rush of modern life, Stoicism becomes a timeless anchor, grounding you in clarity, strength, and serenity.

AS YOU CONTINUE THIS JOURNEY, remember that Stoicism is not about perfection but progress. Each day offers a new opportunity to practice its principles, refine your character, and live with greater purpose. With Stoicism as your guide, you can not only navigate life's challenges but transform them into stepping stones to a more prosperous, more fulfilling existence.

. . .

As Marcus Aurelius wisely observed, *"Waste no more time arguing about what a good man should be. Be one."* Let Stoicism inspire you to live not just a good life but a meaningful and resilient one.

PART II

Stoic Rules to Conquer the Day

In this section, you will be introduced to The Stoic Rules to Conquer the Day. These Stoic Rules will help you to stay focused and productive during the day. It will also help you to better manage your time and energy. By following these rules, you will be able to make the most of each day and reach your goals.

STOIC RULES TO CONQUER
THE DAY

 rafting a Life of Purpose and Resilience

"The happiness of your life depends upon the quality of your thoughts." — Marcus Aurelius

Every day dawns as a blank canvas, waiting for the strokes of our actions, intentions, and thoughts. In the chaos of modern life—overwhelmed by distractions and competing priorities—it's easy to lose sight of what truly matters. But within this whirlwind lies an opportunity: the chance to reclaim our focus, align with our values, and harness each day as a building block for the life we aspire to live.

The Stoics offer timeless principles that are as practical today as 2,000 years ago or longer. Rooted in ancient wisdom, enriched by the science of psychology, and complemented by the transformative power of Positive Mental Attitude (PMA), these rules provide a robust framework for thriving, no matter the circumstances.

HERE ARE the **Stoic Rules to Conquer the Day**—a guide to living with clarity, courage, and purpose.

1. Begin the Day with Gratitude and Purpose

"When you arise in the morning, think of what a privilege it is to be alive, to think, to enjoy, to love." — Marcus Aurelius

MORNINGS ARE SACRED; they set the stage for the hours ahead. How you begin your day influences your mindset, productivity, and interactions. The Stoics understood the power of intentional mornings and used them to align with their values.

MORNING PRACTICE:

• Reflect on three things you are grateful for.

• Set a daily intention: What virtue will guide you today? Patience, courage, focus?

• Visualize potential challenges and prepare your mind to face them with resilience and grace.

Example: Imagine starting your day with gratitude for the warmth of sunlight on your face, the opportunity to learn, and the health of your body. Focusing on these positives creates a mental foundation of abundance, not lack. When you encounter a difficult coworker or a frustrating task, your gratitude fortifies you, allowing you to respond calmly and comfortably.

2. Embrace the Dichotomy of Control

"You have power over your mind—not outside events. Realize this, and you will find strength." — Marcus Aurelius

THE DICHOTOMY of control is a cornerstone of Stoic philosophy. It teaches us to distinguish between what we can control (thoughts, actions, and responses) and what we cannot (external events, others' opinions, and outcomes). By focusing only on what we can control, we free ourselves from unnecessary stress and regain a sense of empowerment.

DAILY PRACTICE:

- Before tackling a task or situation, ask: *What is within my control? What is not?*

- Redirect energy from worrying about the uncontrollable to acting on what you can influence.

EXAMPLE: You're preparing for an important presentation, but technical glitches arise. Instead of panicking, focus on what you can control—your delivery, tone, and message. You will remain composed and effective by channeling your energy into preparation rather than frustration.

. . .

3. Prioritize the Essential

"It is not that we have a short time to live, but that we waste a lot of it." — Seneca

IN THE AGE of constant notifications and endless to-do lists, it's easy to confuse busyness with productivity. Stoicism calls us to discern what truly matters and invest our time and energy in meaningful pursuits.

DAILY PRACTICE:

- Identify your top three priorities for the day.

- Block time for deep, focused work, free from distractions.

- Practice saying "no" to tasks and commitments that don't align with your values or goals.

EXAMPLE: Instead of multitasking between emails, social media, and a critical project, dedicate focused, uninterrupted time to the task that will create the most impact. This singular focus enhances productivity and brings a sense of accomplishment.

4. Master Emotional Regulation

"Keep your emotions in check; nothing great was ever achieved by losing control." — Epictetus

LIFE WILL INEVITABLY THROW challenges your way, but the Stoics remind us that while we cannot control what happens, we can control how we respond. Emotional regulation is the art of pausing, reflecting, and choosing your response rather than reacting impulsively.

DAILY PRACTICE:

- When faced with frustration, pause and breathe deeply.

- Ask yourself: *Is this worth my peace of mind? How can I respond with wisdom?*

- Use mindfulness techniques to ground yourself in the present.

FOR EXAMPLE, **you might react angrily if someone cuts you off in traffic**. Instead, pause, take a deep breath, and let it go. By choosing peace over frustration, you protect your energy and maintain clarity.

5. See Adversity as a Teacher

"The impediment to action advances action. What stands in the way becomes the way." — Marcus Aurelius

EVERY CHALLENGE IS an opportunity for growth. Stoicism sees obstacles not as roadblocks but as stepping stones to resilience, wisdom, and self-improvement.

DAILY PRACTICE:

- Reframe difficulties as lessons: *What can I learn from this?*

- Approach setbacks with curiosity rather than frustration.

EXAMPLE: If you fail to meet a goal, analyze what went wrong. Perhaps you underestimated the time needed or lacked a crucial skill. Use this insight to refine your approach and come back stronger.

6. Act with Integrity and Virtue

"Waste no more time arguing about what a good man should be. Be one." — Marcus Aurelius

Integrity is the bedrock of a meaningful life. The Stoics believed living in alignment with virtues—wisdom, courage, justice, and temperance—creates a life of purpose and peace.

DAILY PRACTICE:

- Before making decisions, ask: *Does this align with my values? Does it reflect the person I aspire to be?*

- Treat others respectfully and fairly, even if they don't reciprocate.

EXAMPLE: Act with integrity when tempted to cut corners at work. Delivering honest, quality work upholds your character and builds trust and respect.

. . .

7. Reflect and Reset at Day's End

"When the light has gone out of sight for you, do not imagine it dead. You may judge the same of yourself." — Seneca

REFLECTION IS a powerful tool for growth. By reviewing your actions, thoughts, and decisions, you can gain clarity on what's working and where you can improve.

EVENING PRACTICE:

• Spend 5–10 minutes reflecting on the day.

• Ask yourself: *What went well? Where did I fall short? What will I do differently tomorrow?*

• Acknowledge your progress and express gratitude for the day's lessons.

EXAMPLE: At night, reflect on a moment when you lost patience. Consider how you could respond more constructively next time. This self-awareness helps you refine your actions and grow in character.

LIVING the Stoic Way

THE STOIC RULES TO Conquer the Day are more than habits—they are a philosophy for life. By beginning each day with gratitude, focusing on what you can control, and acting with integrity, you cultivate a mindset of resilience, purpose, and fulfillment.

INTEGRATING these rules into your daily routine will become second nature, empowering you to navigate challenges with grace and seize opportunities with courage. Let each day be a step toward becoming the person you aspire to be.

REMEMBER **this timeless wisdom from Epictetus**: *"First say to yourself what you would be, and then do what you have to do."*

THE NEXT CHAPTER AWAITS—EXPLORING how these rules can shape your day and your life. Let's embark on this journey together.

THE POWER OF STOIC RULES

A **Framework for Living a Life of Meaning and Mastery**

"ENOUGH IS ENOUGH. There has been enough time for a mediocre life to be lived. Stop waiting. Start living." — Marcus Aurelius

AS THE SUN stretches across the horizon each morning, a silent question greets us: *What will you do with this day?* The answer to this

question defines more than just the next 24 hours—it shapes who we are, who we are becoming, and the legacy we'll leave behind. Yet, too often, we squander this opportunity, distracted by trivialities, paralyzed by doubt, or numbed by routine.

THE STOIC RULES are not abstract ideals confined to ancient philosophy but tools forged in the fires of life's challenges. They call us to action, urging us to wake up, take charge, and transform our days into stepping stones toward a life of purpose, strength, and fulfillment. Infused with the principles of Stoicism, the optimism of Positive Mental Attitude (PMA), and insights from psychology, these rules offer clarity and resilience.

1. Treat Time as the Essence of Life

"You are not spending time; you are spending your life." — Seneca

PICTURE TIME as a vast ocean and each moment as a drop. Once the drop slips away, it cannot be reclaimed. Seneca's words remind us that every hour wasted is an irreplaceable fragment of life lost. The question is not how much time you have—it's how wisely you use it.

STORY: There's a tale of a farmer who asked a wise sage how to find more time in his day. The sage handed him a simple jar filled with rocks, pebbles, and sand. "The rocks," the sage explained, "are your priorities—family, health, purpose. The pebbles are your tasks. The sand? Distractions." The farmer realized the jar could only hold so much. If you fill it with sand first, there's no room for the rocks.

. . .

ACTIONABLE RULE: Each morning, identify your "rocks"—the tasks that truly matter—and give them your undivided attention. Let the sand (distractions) come later, if at all.

2. Begin and End with Gratitude

"Gratitude turns what we have into enough." — Epictetus

GRATITUDE IS the gateway to abundance. It shifts your mindset from what's lacking to what's present, from frustration to fulfillment. Gratitude is not just a "feel-good" practice—it's a scientifically proven tool for enhancing well-being and resilience.

STORY: Despite being emperor of Rome, Marcus Aurelius often reflected on life's simple blessings. In his journal, he expressed gratitude for the mentors who shaped him, the friends who supported him, and even the adversaries who tested his patience. Gratitude, for him, was not just a thought but a practice of presence.

ACTIONABLE RULE:

- Each morning, write down three things you're grateful for.

- Each evening, reflect on one lesson or joy from the day.

EXAMPLE: Be thankful for the warmth of your bed, the kindness of a stranger, or the resilience you showed in a difficult moment.

. . .

3. Embrace the Power of Control

"You have power over your mind—not outside events. Realize this, and you will find strength." — Marcus Aurelius

THE STOIC PRINCIPLE of the Dichotomy of Control shields against unnecessary suffering. It teaches us to focus on what we can control—our actions, thoughts, and attitudes—while releasing the rest.

STORY: Epictetus, born into slavery, had every reason to feel powerless. Yet, he chose to focus not on his circumstances but on his inner freedom. His resilience turned him into one of history's most revered philosophers.

ACTIONABLE RULE:

• When faced with stress, ask yourself: *"Is this within my control?"* If not, let it go.

• Shift your energy toward actions and thoughts that align with your values.

EXAMPLE: If a flight is delayed, focus on how to use the time productively—read, reflect, or call a loved one.

4. Seek Discomfort to Find Growth

"The impediment to action advances action. What stands in the way becomes the way." — Marcus Aurelius

CHALLENGES ARE NOT ROADBLOCKS—THEY are staircases to your higher self. Each obstacle you face sharpens your skills, strengthens your character, and deepens your wisdom.

STORY: Cato the Younger, a Stoic senator, deliberately walked barefoot and wore plain clothing in public to build resilience against ridicule. By embracing discomfort, he gained an unshakable confidence.

ACTIONABLE RULE: Each day, step outside your comfort zone.

EXAMPLE: If you fear public speaking, start small—share your thoughts in a team meeting. Growth thrives in discomfort.

5. Respond with Virtue, Not Impulse

"It's not what happens to you, but how you react to it that matters." — Epictetus

REACTIVITY IS A THIEF—IT steals your peace and clouds your judgment. Stoicism teaches us to pause, reflect, and respond with integrity.

. . .

STORY: Socrates, after being mocked by an angry critic, smiled and said, "He insults me because he does not know me well enough to find my true flaws." His calmness disarmed the attacker and preserved his peace.

ACTIONABLE RULE:

- When provoked, pause. Breathe deeply and ask yourself: *"What is the most virtuous response?"*

EXAMPLE: If someone rebukes you, thank them for their perspective and reflect on what you can learn.

6. Reflect, Refine, and Recalibrate

"An unexamined life is not worth living." — Socrates

REFLECTION IS the compass that keeps you aligned with your values and goals. It transforms mistakes into lessons and intentions into actions.

STORY: Seneca advised his followers to reflect nightly, asking: *"What did I do well? Where did I fall short? What will I do differently tomorrow?"* This practice turned minor adjustments into monumental growth.

ACTIONABLE RULE: Dedicate five minutes each evening to review your day:

1 What did I accomplish?
2 Where did I struggle?
3 What will I improve tomorrow?

EXAMPLE: If you lose patience during a tense moment, plan to approach similar situations calmly and clearly.

THE BRIDGE to the Next Chapter: Building Inner Freedom

THE STOIC RULES are not mere suggestions but a way of life. They challenge you to live deliberately, to find strength in adversity, and to transform each day into a masterpiece of purpose and virtue.

BUT THE JOURNEY doesn't end here. As you integrate these principles, you'll discover a more profound truth: true freedom is not found in external circumstances but within your mind.

> *"Today, choose to be the architect of your life. Waste no more time waiting for ideal conditions—create them. Live each moment with intention, and let these rules guide you to a life well-lived."*

IN THE NEXT CHAPTER, we will delve deeper into inner freedom—how to break free from the chains of fear, doubt, and external validation to live a life of authenticity and peace. Let's continue this journey together.

STOIC RULES FOR TODAY

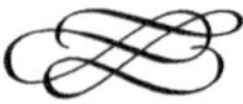

𝒶 Blueprint for a Purposeful Life

"If you want to escape the things that harass you, what you need is not to be in a different place but to be a different person." — Seneca

Every sunrise carries a promise: the opportunity to rewrite your story, reshape your mindset, and live purposefully. Today is not just another day—it's a gift, a challenge, and a canvas. Stoicism invites us to approach life not with resignation but with resolve. It calls us to

rise above the noise of distractions and doubts and take control of our inner world.

THESE **STOIC RULES for Today** serve as your compass, offering timeless principles to help you navigate challenges, harness your potential, and cultivate a meaningful life. Each rule gives you the tools to transform ordinary moments into extraordinary opportunities.

1. Seek Discomfort, Embrace Growth

"Difficulties strengthen the mind, as labor does the body." — Seneca

GROWTH DOESN'T COME from staying within the boundaries of comfort but from stepping into the unknown. Every challenge you face invites you to grow stronger, wiser, and more resilient.

STORY: When Marcus Aurelius faced the pressures of leading an empire, he didn't complain about the weight of his responsibilities. Instead, he saw them as opportunities to practice patience, wisdom, and courage. His journal, *Meditations*, reflects this mindset: *"The impediment to action advances action. What stands in the way becomes the way."*

ACTIONABLE RULE: Each day, choose one task that makes you uncomfortable—starting a tough conversation, tackling a new skill, or facing a fear. Growth lives on the other side of discomfort.

. . .

Example: If public speaking terrifies you, volunteer to share your thoughts in a team meeting. With each step, you'll expand your comfort zone.

2. Guard Your Time and Energy

"It is not that we have a short time to live, but that we waste a lot of it." — Seneca

Time is your most precious resource. How you spend it shapes the life you build. Don't squander it on trivialities or people who drain your energy.

Story: Epictetus, born into slavery, had little control over his circumstances but absolute control over how he spent his time and energy. He dedicated himself to mastering his thoughts and actions, becoming a celebrated philosopher.

Actionable Rule: Evaluate your commitments. Say "no" to anything that doesn't align with your values or goals. Protect your time fiercely, as if it were gold.

Reflection: Ask yourself, "Does this activity bring me closer to my purpose, or is it a distraction?"

3. Take Responsibility for Your Emotions

"You may not control all the events that happen to you, but you can decide not to be reduced by them." — Maya Angelou

NO ONE CAN MAKE you angry, sad, or frustrated unless you allow them to. Emotional control is the cornerstone of mental freedom.

STORY: Imagine a stormy sea. The waves may be chaotic, but the deep waters remain calm. Stoicism teaches us to be like the ocean—steady and composed, regardless of surface turbulence.

ACTIONABLE RULE: When faced with a challenging situation, pause and ask yourself: *"Am I reacting emotionally or responding thoughtfully?"* Take a deep breath and reclaim your power.

EXAMPLE: Respond calmly and gracefully instead of snapping at a rude colleague. This will preserve your peace and set an example of strength.

4. Break Free from Vice and Temptation

"No man is free who is not master of himself." — Epictetus

VICES—WHETHER overindulgence, procrastination, or negativity—are chains that limit your potential. Freedom begins with self-discipline.

. . .

Story: Cato the Younger, a Stoic leader, practiced self-control by deliberately wearing simple clothing and living modestly. By resisting societal temptations, he strengthened his inner resolve.

Actionable Rule: Identify one habit holding you back and replace it with a healthier alternative.

Example: If you tend to overindulge in social media, set a timer for 15 minutes. Use the saved time to meditate, journal, or exercise.

5. Live with Purpose and Virtue

"Waste no more time arguing about what a good man should be. Be one." — Marcus Aurelius

Purpose is your guiding star; virtue is your compass. Together, they lead you toward a meaningful life.

Story: Zeno of Citium, the founder of Stoicism, lost everything in a shipwreck. Instead of despairing, he dedicated his life to teaching others how to live virtuously. His loss became the foundation of his purpose.

Actionable Rule: Each morning, set a purpose for your day. Ask yourself, "What virtue will I practice today—courage, patience, kindness?" Let this question guide your actions.

. . .

EXAMPLE: If you want to lead with kindness, genuinely thank someone who often goes unnoticed—you know who that might be.

6. Turn Adversity into Advantage

"The fire that makes the blade sharpens the sword." — Marcus Aurelius

LIFE WILL THROW obstacles your way. The Stoic mindset transforms these obstacles into opportunities for growth.

STORY: Seneca once wrote, *"A gem cannot be polished without friction, nor a man perfected without trials."* He believed that hardship was the crucible of greatness.

ACTIONABLE RULE: When adversity strikes, ask yourself: *"What lesson can I learn from this? How can I use it to grow?"*

EXAMPLE: If a project fails, view it as feedback. Analyze what went wrong and use those insights to improve your next attempt.

7. Reflect and Refine Each Evening

"Examine yourself, and see what is within you that makes you weak, and what that makes you strong." — Epictetus

REFLECTION IS NOT about dwelling on mistakes but learning from them. By examining your day, you prepare for a better tomorrow.

STORY: At the end of each day, Marcus Aurelius would review his actions, asking himself whether he lived in alignment with his values. This nightly ritual honed his character.

ACTIONABLE RULE: Dedicate 5–10 minutes before bed to reflect on your day:

• *What did I do well today?*
• *Where can I improve?*
• *What will I do differently tomorrow?*

EXAMPLE: If you have lost patience with a loved one or anyone, reflect on why. Then, plan how to approach similar situations with empathy and calmness.

THE POWER of Intentional Living

THE STOIC RULES are more than guidelines—they're a way of life. They remind us that greatness is not achieved through grand gestures but through daily actions, small choices, and quiet resolve.

EVERY MOMENT IS an opportunity to grow, to act with integrity, and to align with your higher self. As you integrate these principles into your day, you'll notice a shift—not just in how you live but in how you see yourself and the world around you.

. . .

"The happiness of your life depends upon the quality of your thoughts." — Marcus Aurelius

Now, let us move on to the next chapter, where we will explore six Stoic Rules and how to apply these principles to cultivate a life of inner freedom and lasting fulfillment. Let's continue this journey together.

RULE NUMBER 1: LIVING IN ACCORDANCE WITH NATURE

_L_iving in Accordance with Nature

"This thou must always bear in mind, what is the nature of the whole, and what is my nature."
— _Marcus Aurelius, Meditations_

THE STOICS BELIEVED nature was the blueprint for a fulfilling and virtuous life. They argued that understanding one's nature is understanding one's role within the grand tapestry of the universe. For the Stoics, "nature" was not merely about the environment or the physical world—it was a philosophy of life, a guide to navigating existence with wisdom, clarity, and purpose.

THE STOIC PERSPECTIVE **on Nature**

. . .

THE STOICS UNDERSTOOD nature as the fundamental principles governing the universe and everything within it. They viewed the cosmos as an interconnected, harmonious system governed by the *Logos*, a divine intelligence that permeates all existence. This Logos, they believed, gave meaning, order, and purpose to every aspect of the universe—from the tiniest atom to the vast expanse of galaxies.

FOR THE STOICS, the human mind and soul were extensions of this divine Logos. Our ability to reason, reflect, and choose virtuous actions was seen as a gift of divine intelligence. Therefore, to live by nature meant aligning one's actions, thoughts, and values with this universal intelligence. It meant understanding that we are not isolated but integral parts of a greater whole.

MARCUS AURELIUS BEAUTIFULLY captures this interconnectedness: *"What brings no benefit to the hive brings none to the bee."* This insight reminds us that our lives gain meaning through our connection to others and our alignment with the natural order.

LIVING IN HARMONY WITH NATURE: The Stoic Way

THE STOICS TAUGHT that to live in harmony with nature; we must embrace its laws and accept the reality of what we cannot control. In doing so, we can cultivate virtues such as wisdom, courage, justice, and self-control, which allow us to thrive even in adversity.

1. Accepting the Natural Order

. . .

STOICISM TEACHES us that life is filled with events beyond our control —illness, death, loss, and natural disasters are all part of the natural order. Resisting these realities only leads to suffering. Instead, the Stoics emphasized the importance of focusing on what we *can* control: our thoughts, actions, and attitudes.

EXAMPLE: Imagine facing a sudden job loss. You cannot change the circumstances but choose how to respond. A Stoic would accept the event without resentment and channel their energy into what they can control, such as learning new skills, seeking opportunities, and maintaining a positive outlook.

AS EPICTETUS SAID, *"It's not what happens to you, but how you react to it that matters."*

2. Practicing Virtues as a Path to Harmony

THE STOICS BELIEVED that living in harmony with nature required cultivating virtues. These virtues are not abstract ideals; they are practical tools for navigating life's challenges:

• **Wisdom** helps us discern what is truly important.
• **Courage** empowers us to face difficulties with strength.
• **Justice** ensures we act pretty and honorably toward others.
• **Self-control** helps us resist harmful desires and maintain balance.

EXAMPLE: Consider a situation where someone wrongs you. Wisdom allows you to see the bigger picture and avoid acting out of anger.

Courage gives you the strength to forgive, while justice guides you to respond with fairness. Self-control ensures you don't retaliate in a way that compromises your character.

BY PRACTICING THESE VIRTUES, the Stoics believed we could lead lives of purpose, resilience, and tranquility.

THE INTERCONNECTEDNESS of All Things

STOIC PHILOSOPHY CENTERS on the idea that everything in the universe is interconnected and interdependent. Just as rivers flow into oceans and trees depend on sunlight, humans are also connected to the natural world.

MARCUS AURELIUS REMINDS US: *"The universe is change; our life is what our thoughts make it."* This idea underscores that we are not isolated individuals but part of a greater whole. Our actions ripple outward, influencing the world in ways we may never fully understand.

EXAMPLE: A simple act of kindness—a smile, a helping hand— may brighten someone's day and inspire them to pass it on. These small moments of compassion remind us of our shared humanity and responsibility to contribute positively to the collective.

LIVING in Accordance with Nature

TO LIVE in harmony with nature is to embrace life as it is rather than as we wish it to be. It's about aligning our actions with the natural order and striving to fulfill our unique role within the universe.

PRACTICAL STEPS TO Align with Nature:

1 Focus on What You Can Control

Let go of worries about external events and focus on your thoughts and actions. While you cannot control the weather, you can choose how to dress for it.

2 Cultivate Gratitude

Appreciate your blessings. Life is fleeting, and what you take for granted today may be gone tomorrow.

3 Practice Patience and Acceptance

When faced with difficulties, remember that they are part of life's natural rhythm. Acceptance is the first step to finding peace.

4 Act with Purpose and Integrity

Live each day with intention, ensuring your actions align with your values and contribute to the greater good.

5 Build Resilience

Strengthen your mind and character through challenges. Each obstacle is an opportunity to grow stronger and wiser.

6 Nurture Connections

Recognize your interdependence with others. Foster relationships built on empathy, respect, and mutual support.

Nature as a Teacher

For the Stoics, nature was more than a concept—it was a teacher. Observing the natural world teaches us balance, patience, and resilience.

- **The River's Flow**: A river does not resist obstacles; it flows around them. Similarly, we should adapt to life's challenges rather than resist them.

- **The Tree's Strength**: A tree grows stronger by weathering storms. In the same way, adversity can strengthen our character and resilience.
  - **The Cycle of Seasons**: Nature's cycles remind us that life is ever-changing. By embracing change, we can find peace in life's impermanence.

The Power of Living in Harmony with Nature

Living in accordance with nature is not about retreating to the wilderness or rejecting modern life. It's about aligning with the natural order, practicing virtue, and embracing the interconnectedness of all things.

When we live in harmony with nature, we cultivate a sense of purpose and fulfillment. We let go of unnecessary anxieties, focus on what truly matters, and contribute positively to the world.

. . .

As Marcus Aurelius reminds us, *"You have power over your mind—not outside events. Realize this, and you will find strength."* By understanding our nature and our role within the greater whole, we unlock the wisdom, courage, and peace needed to live fully and virtuously.

Let us walk this path with intention, embracing the teachings of nature as our guide.

RULE NUMBER 2: FOCUS ON WHAT'S WITHIN YOUR CONTROL

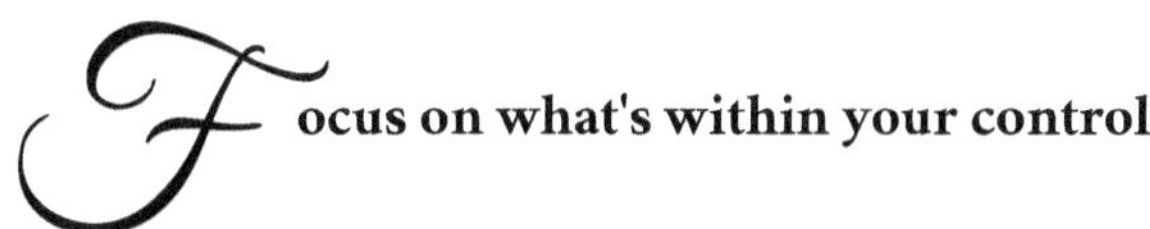 **ocus on what's within your control**

"You have power over your mind - not outside events. Realize this, and you will find strength."
— *Marcus Aurelius, Meditations*

IT'S easy to fall victim to a whirlwind of negativity when things don't go our way. We allow ourselves to be dragged into thoughts about things we cannot control—our failures, fears, and all the "what ifs" of the future. This habit of mental drifting often triggers feelings of helplessness, anxiety, and even despair as we become trapped in a cycle of rumination and worry. But the truth is, we have far more power than we give ourselves credit for.

THE STOIC EMPEROR Marcus Aurelius reminds us of a profound truth: we are not helpless victims of external events but **the architects of our internal world.**

. . .

Breaking Free from the Cycle of Negative Thinking

WHEN LIFE FEELS OVERWHELMING, our minds often gravitate toward the negative—what we've lost, what we fear, and what might go wrong next. This pattern drains our energy and clouds our ability to reason.

As NEUROPSYCHOLOGIST DR. SHANNON IRVINE explains, *"Thoughts fire before emotion, and then your brain connects. If you repeat that link enough, it will start running automatically."* In other words, our thoughts directly shape our emotions. If we dwell on negative thoughts, we create a negative emotional state. But the reverse is also true—when we consciously redirect our thoughts, we can cultivate positive emotions and a more evident mindset.

The Power of Three Questions

WHEN YOU FEEL yourself slipping into negative thinking, pause and ask:

1 What worries me?
2 What is under my control?
3 What matters most to me, and what can I do?

THIS SIMPLE PRACTICE brings your focus back to the present and empowers you to take action where it truly matters.

. . .

The Dichotomy of Control: A Life-Changing Principle

Epictetus wrote in *A Manual for Living*: *"Happiness and freedom begin with a clear understanding of one principle: Some things are within our control, and some things are not. The chief task in life is to identify and separate matters to tell me which externalities are not under my control and which have to do with my choices."*

This principle forms the cornerstone of Stoic philosophy and is just as relevant today as 2,000 years ago.

What You Can Control:

• Your beliefs, attitudes, and mindset
• Your habits and how you spend your time
• Your goals and the effort you put into them
• Your responses to challenges and setbacks
• Your health choices, such as diet, sleep, and exercise

What You Can't Control:

• Other people's opinions, actions, or emotions
• The weather, economy, or external circumstances
• The outcome of your efforts
• The past and the uncertainties of the future

. . .

WHEN YOU FOCUS on what you can control, you reclaim your power. When you obsess over what you cannot, you waste energy and create unnecessary suffering.

EXAMPLE: If you're stuck in traffic and running late for an important meeting, you cannot control the traffic. But you *can* control how you respond. Instead of stressing, use the time to prepare mentally for the meeting, listen to an inspiring podcast, or practice mindfulness.

THE PRESENT MOMENT: Where Strength Lies

A COMMON TRAP of the mind is living in the future—imagining worst-case scenarios, worrying about what might happen, and playing out endless "what ifs." But the future is an illusion; it hasn't happened yet. The only reality is the present moment.

FOCUSING on the here and now allows you to regain control, shifting from powerless worry to purposeful action.

EXAMPLE: If you're worried about losing your job, focus on what you can do today instead of dwelling on fears of unemployment. Update your resume, network with colleagues, or learn a new skill. These small, actionable steps empower you and reduce anxiety.

As Marcus Aurelius wrote: *"Confine yourself to the present."*

The Strength of Gratitude and Positive Focus

Gratitude is one of the most powerful tools for shifting one's mindset. Focusing on what one has instead of what one lacks cultivates a positive mental attitude (PMA) that encourages resilience and joy.

Daily Practice:

• Each morning, write down three things you're grateful for.
• At night, reflect on one positive thing that happened during the day.

Example: On a stressful day, you might feel grateful for something as simple as a warm cup of tea, a kind word from a friend, or the beauty of a sunset. These small moments remind you of life's abundance and help ground you in positivity.

Owning Your Choices and Reclaiming Freedom

The Stoics teach us that while we can't control life's events, we can control how we perceive and respond to them. **Your response is your freedom.**

Practical Steps to Own Your Choices:

1 **Examine Your Behavior:** Reflect on where you're succeeding and where you're falling short. Growth comes from honest self-awareness.

2 Take Action, Not Blame: When faced with a challenge, focus on solutions rather than dwelling on the problem.

3 Let Go of Outcomes: Do your best, but detach from the results. Accept that some things are beyond your influence.

EXAMPLE: If you dislike your job, focus on what you can control instead of complaining. Use the opportunity to build new skills, network, or plan your transition to a more fulfilling role.

LIVING in the Eternal Sunshine State of Mind

MARCUS AURELIUS WROTE, *"The soul becomes dyed with the color of its thoughts."* Your thoughts shape your reality. You create a life filled with purpose and peace by consciously choosing thoughts of strength, gratitude, and possibility.

THE MINDSET OF CONTROL:

- Accept what you cannot change with grace.
- Focus your energy on what you *can* change.
- Practice gratitude daily to ground yourself in the positive.
- Take small, meaningful actions toward your goals.

EXAMPLE: If your goal is better health, focus on the choices you control: eat nutritious meals, exercise regularly, and get enough sleep. Celebrate small wins, like completing a workout or preparing a healthy dish, as steps toward your larger goal.

. . .

STRENGTH LIES Within

LIFE WILL ALWAYS PRESENT CHALLENGES. But as Marcus Aurelius reminds us, your strength lies not in controlling the uncontrollable but in mastering your mind. When you focus on what you can control —your thoughts, actions, and responses—you unlock the power to navigate life's uncertainties with grace and resilience.

EVERY DAY, you have a choice: will you let external events dictate your happiness, or will you take control of your mind and create peace?

REMEMBER: **You have power over your mind, not outside events. Realize this, and you will find strength. Use that strength** to build the life you deserve.

RULE NUMBER 3: CULTIVATE GRATITUDE

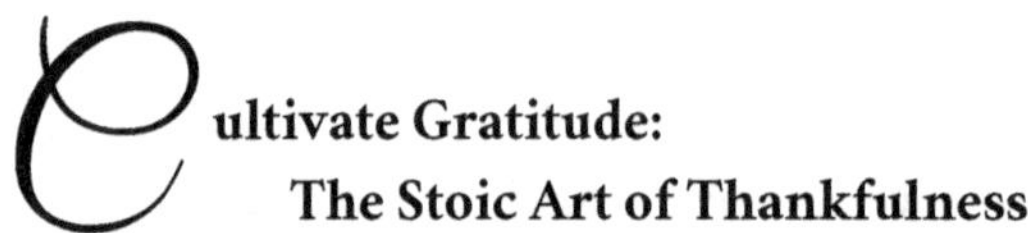

ultivate Gratitude:
The Stoic Art of Thankfulness

"Gratitude is not only the greatest of virtues but the parent of all others." —
Cicero

GRATITUDE IS MORE than a polite "thank you" or a fleeting moment of appreciation; it is a state of being, a mindset, and a practice. Derived from the Latin word *gratia*, meaning grace or thankfulness, gratitude is a bridge between ourselves and the world, connecting us to the beauty, lessons, and blessings life offers—even in its most challenging moments.

THE STOICS, masters of introspection and resilience, regarded gratitude as fundamental to living a meaningful life. They believed practicing gratitude could unlock more profound contentment, joy, and a clearer sense of purpose. Modern psychology echoes this wisdom, demonstrating appreciation enhances mental health and fosters stronger relationships and physical well-being. But what makes gratitude so powerful? And how can we cultivate it in our daily lives?

THE STOIC FOUNDATION **of Gratitude**

"He is a wise man who does not grieve for the things which he has not, but rejoices for those which he has." — Epictetus

FOR THE STOICS, gratitude wasn't limited to appreciating the good times—it was about embracing the entirety of life, including its hardships. They taught that everything we have, from material possessions to the people in our lives, is fleeting and should be cherished while it lasts. Gratitude, in their view, was the antidote to entitlement and dissatisfaction.

EPICTETUS, a formerly enslaved person turned philosopher, exemplified this mindset. He urged his students to focus on what they could control—their thoughts, actions, and responses—and to be thankful for the opportunities life presented, even in adversity. For the Stoics, gratitude was not just a reaction to positive experiences but a proactive practice of recognizing the value in all aspects of life.

GRATITUDE AS A DAILY **Practice**

"When you arise in the morning, think of what a privilege it is to be alive, to think, to enjoy, to love." — Marcus Aurelius

. . .

GRATITUDE IS NOT AN ABSTRACT CONCEPT; we can cultivate it daily. The following practices, inspired by Stoic wisdom and modern psychology, can help you embrace gratitude as a way of life.

1. Practice Negative Visualization

THE STOICS BELIEVED that to appreciate what we have, we must first imagine life without it. Negative visualization involves reflecting on the loss of something we hold dear—our health, loved ones, or even simple comforts. By imagining these losses, we awaken a deeper appreciation for their presence.

STORY: Marcus Aurelius, in his *Meditations*, would remind himself of the impermanence of life. He wrote: *"You could leave life right now. Let that determine what you do and say and think."* This awareness deepened his gratitude for every fleeting moment.

ACTIONABLE PRACTICE: Take a moment each day to imagine life without something or someone you cherish. Then, please return to the present and appreciate their presence with renewed gratitude.

2. Reflect on Your Blessings

"Gratitude turns what we have into enough." — Anonymous

IT'S easy to focus on what's lacking, but gratitude redirects our attention to what's already abundant in our lives. Reflecting on your blessings—no matter how small—cultivates a positive mental attitude (PMA) and reduces stress.

STORY: Seneca often advised his peers to find joy in simplicity, such as the warmth of the sun or the sound of a loved one's laughter. These small acknowledgments, he believed, were the foundation of happiness.

ACTIONABLE PRACTICE: Each morning, list three things you're grateful for. They could be as simple as a good night's sleep, a delicious meal, or a kind word from a friend.

3. Gratitude Through Self-Reflection

"The unexamined life is not worth living." — Socrates

GRATITUDE ISN'T JUST about external blessings—it's also about recognizing your growth and the choices that have led you to where you are. You foster a sense of empowerment and thankfulness by reflecting on your actions and their positive outcomes.

STORY: Epictetus encouraged his students to reflect on their progress and choices, emphasizing that gratitude begins with acknowledging one's efforts and resilience.

ACTIONABLE PRACTICE: At the end of each day, ask yourself:

• *What am I proud of today?*
• *What small victories have I achieved?*
• *How have my actions contributed to the good in my life or others?*

4. Acknowledge the Interconnectedness of Life

"We are like branches on a tree, connected by the roots of humanity." —
Seneca

THE STOICS EMPHASIZED the interconnectedness of all things. Gratitude grows when we recognize how much we owe to others— the kindness of a stranger, the support of loved ones, or even the farmer who grew the food on our plate.

STORY: Marcus Aurelius often reflected on how his existence was shaped by countless others, from his teachers to the soldiers who protected Rome. This awareness deepened his gratitude and humility.

ACTIONABLE PRACTICE: Thank someone who has positively impacted your life. A handwritten note, a heartfelt conversation, or even a small act of kindness can strengthen your relationships and spread positivity.

5. Gratitude in Adversity

"A gem cannot be polished without friction, nor a man perfected without trials." — Seneca

. . .

GRATITUDE DOESN'T MEAN IGNORING life's difficulties but finding value in them. While uncomfortable, challenges are opportunities for growth, resilience, and perspective.

STORY: When faced with exile, Seneca didn't wallow in self-pity. Instead, he used the time to write and reflect, producing some of his most profound works. He viewed his hardship as a teacher, not a punishment.

ACTIONABLE PRACTICE: The next time you face a challenge, ask yourself: *"What can I learn from this? How can this make me stronger?"* Gratitude for adversity transforms obstacles into opportunities.

THE SCIENCE of Gratitude

MODERN PSYCHOLOGY REINFORCES what the Stoics taught centuries ago. Studies show gratitude improves mental health, enhances relationships, and boosts physical well-being. People who regularly express gratitude report better sleep, reduced stress, and increased happiness.

FROM A PSYCHOLOGICAL PERSPECTIVE, gratitude activates the brain's reward centers, releasing dopamine and serotonin—neurotransmitters associated with pleasure and well-being. Over time, gratitude rewires your brain to focus on the positive, creating a virtuous cycle of contentment.

. . .

A Life of Grateful Living

GRATITUDE IS NOT JUST a fleeting emotion; it's a way of being. It's the practice of seeing the extraordinary in the ordinary, finding beauty in imperfection, and cherishing the fleeting moments that make life meaningful.

REFLECTION: Think about the beauty of a sunset, the laughter of a child, or the quiet comfort of a warm cup of tea. These are life's simple yet profound blessings. Please take a moment to savor them.

EMBRACING gratitude daily creates a more profound sense of fulfillment and joy. As Marcus Aurelius reminds us, *"When you arise in the morning, think of what a privilege it is to be alive, to think, to enjoy, to love."*

GRATITUDE IS a compass that guides you back to what truly matters. Let it illuminate your path as we explore, in the next chapter, how to transform obstacles into opportunities through the Stoic art of resilience. The journey continues.

RULE NUMBER 4: EMBRACE ADVERSITY

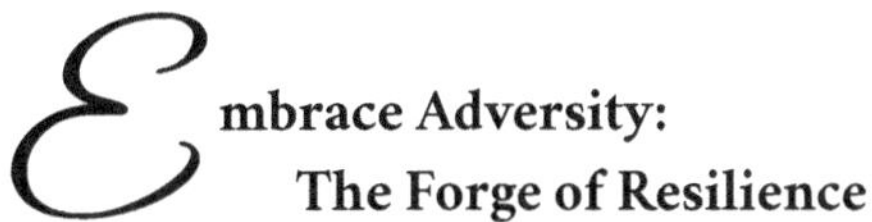

mbrace Adversity:
The Forge of Resilience

"The impediment to action advances action. What stands in the way becomes the way." — Marcus Aurelius

ADVERSITY IS an inevitable companion on life's journey. It knocks on the doors of emperors and commoners, testing character, patience, and resolve. For Marcus Aurelius, one of history's greatest Stoic philosophers, adversity was not an enemy but a teacher, a necessary crucible for growth. He didn't merely endure hardship—he embraced it, transforming it into a source of wisdom and strength.

ADVERSITY IS NOT JUST an external force; often, it resides within us. Our doubts, fears, and untrained minds can be our most formidable adversaries. Yet, as Marcus Aurelius teaches, our most significant power lies in our ability to govern our responses and master our inner world.

THIS CHAPTER INVITES you to redefine your relationship with hardship and see adversity not as an obstacle but as an opportunity to grow, strengthen your character, and live a more meaningful life.

THE GIFT of Adversity

"What we fear doing most is usually what we most need to do." — Ralph Waldo Emerson

ADVERSITY STRIPS AWAY PRETENSE, forcing us to confront our deepest fears, limitations, and vulnerabilities. It compels us to ask difficult questions: *What do I truly value? What am I willing to fight for? How do I move forward when the road is unclear?*

MARCUS AURELIUS RULED during great turmoil—plagues, wars, and political betrayals. Yet he never allowed external chaos to rob him of inner peace. In his private journal, *Meditations*, he wrote, *"You have power over your mind—not outside events. Realize this, and you will find strength."*

HIS WORDS REMIND us that adversity is not about what happens to us but how we respond to it. Every challenge offers an opportunity for growth.

TRANSFORMING ADVERSITY INTO STRENGTH

1. Accept What You Cannot Control

"You may not control all the events that happen to you, but you can decide not to be reduced by them." — Maya Angelou

AT THE HEART of Stoic philosophy is the principle of the **Dichotomy of Control**: focus on what you can control and release what you cannot. Adversity often arises from situations outside our influence—illness, loss, betrayal. By accepting these realities, we free ourselves from unnecessary suffering and direct our energy toward constructive action.

EXAMPLE: When Marcus Aurelius faced betrayal from close allies, he didn't waste time lamenting their actions. Instead, he focused on maintaining his integrity and serving his empire.

ACTIONABLE RULE: When faced with adversity, ask yourself:

- *What is within my control?*
- *What is beyond my control?*

FOCUS on what you can change and let go of the rest.

2. Cultivate Resilience

"Adversity introduces a man to himself." — Albert Einstein

. . .

Resilience is the ability to bounce back from setbacks and persist in facing difficulty. It's not about avoiding hardship but building the mental and emotional strength to navigate it.

Story: Epictetus, born into slavery, endured immense suffering in his early life. Yet he refused to let his circumstances define him. Through philosophy, he transformed his pain into wisdom, teaching others that true freedom lies in mastering one's mind.

Actionable Practice: Develop a **Growth Mindset**, as coined by psychologist Carol Dweck. View challenges as opportunities to learn and grow rather than insurmountable obstacles.

Example: If you fail at a project, instead of seeing it as a personal failure, analyze what went wrong, identify lessons, and use them to improve your future efforts.

3. Engage in Self-Reflection

"Know thyself." — Delphic maxim

Self-reflection is a powerful tool for navigating adversity. By examining our thoughts, emotions, and actions, we gain clarity on our strengths and areas for improvement. This introspection helps us respond to challenges with wisdom rather than impulse.

. . .

Story: Marcus Aurelius practiced nightly self-reflection, reviewing his actions and asking whether they aligned with his values. This habit strengthened his character and prepared him for future challenges.

Actionable Practice: At the end of each day, ask yourself:

- *How did I respond to today's challenges?*
- *What did I learn about myself?*
- *How can I improve tomorrow?*

4. Seek Support, Not Solitude

"Strength was knowing when to ask for help and not being too proud to do it."
— Karen Marie Moning

Stoicism is often misunderstood as a solitary, emotionless philosophy. In reality, the Stoics valued community and recognized the importance of seeking support during difficult times.

Story: Marcus Aurelius relied on trusted advisors and friends even as emperor. He understood that strength lies not in isolation but in connection.

Actionable Rule: When adversity strikes, don't hesitate to contact a friend, mentor, or counselor. Sharing your struggles lightens the burden and often reveals new perspectives and solutions.

. . .

5. See Challenges as Teachers

"A gem cannot be polished without friction, nor a man perfected without trials." — Seneca

ADVERSITY IS life's most excellent teacher. Every setback, failure, or hardship carries a lesson waiting to be discovered. By embracing this mindset, you transform obstacles into stepping stones toward growth.

STORY: Nelson Mandela spent 27 years in prison, enduring unimaginable hardship. Yet he emerged with a spirit of forgiveness and a vision for a united South Africa. His adversity became the foundation for his greatness.

ACTIONABLE PRACTICE: When faced with a challenge, pause and ask yourself:

• *What can I learn from this?*
• *How can this make me stronger or wiser?*

EXAMPLE: If you're navigating a complicated relationship, consider it an opportunity to practice patience, empathy, and communication.

ADVERSITY as the Path to Fulfillment

"The best revenge is not to be like your enemy." — Marcus Aurelius

. . .

ADVERSITY CAN SHAPE US, refine us, and reveal our inner strength. It reminds us that life's most significant victories often come from its most brutal battles. As Marcus Aurelius wrote, *"What stands in the way becomes the way."*

WE CAN TURN adversity into an ally by accepting what we cannot control, cultivating resilience, engaging in self-reflection, seeking support, and learning from challenges. Each hardship becomes a stepping stone to personal growth, resilience, and fulfillment.

EMBRACING adversity doesn't mean seeking it out—it means facing it with courage, wisdom, and grace when it arises. It's about choosing to grow rather than shrink, to act rather than despair.

AS WE TRANSITION to the next chapter, let us carry forward the Stoic lesson that adversity can be transformed into an opportunity for greatness when met with the right mindset. Now, let's explore how to channel this resilience into cultivating a life of purpose and meaning. The journey continues.

RULE NUMBER 5: PRACTICE SELF-DISCIPLINE

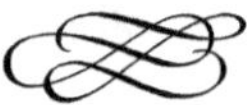

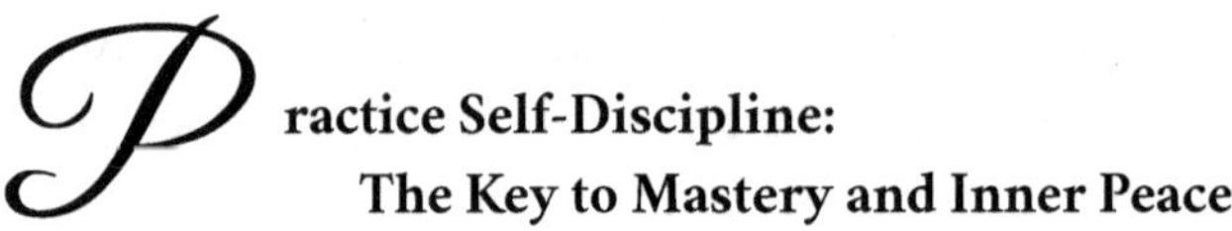

ractice Self-Discipline:
The Key to Mastery and Inner Peace

"If you are distressed by anything external, the pain is not due to the thing itself, but to your estimate of it; and this you have the power to revoke at any moment." — Marcus Aurelius

SELF-DISCIPLINE IS the quiet engine behind every meaningful achievement, a force that elevates ordinary lives to extraordinary ones. It is the invisible thread connecting ambition to reality, the bridge between where you are now and where you aspire to be. For Marcus Aurelius, self-discipline was more than a tool—a way of life.

AS ONE OF the most powerful men in the world at the time, Marcus Aurelius could have indulged in every luxury and whim. Yet, as a devoted practitioner of Stoicism, he chose to live a life guided by principles rather than impulses. His journal Meditations distilled timeless lessons on self-discipline, offering a roadmap to master our thoughts, emotions, and actions.

THIS CHAPTER EXPLORES PRACTICAL, powerful ways to cultivate self-discipline, weaving in lessons from Stoicism, Positive Mental Attitude (PMA), and psychology. Let's delve into how to build the mental fortitude that shapes not just a day but an entire lifetime.

1. Find Your Purpose: The Foundation of Self-Discipline

"The object of life is not to be on the side of the majority, but to escape finding oneself in the ranks of the insane." — Marcus Aurelius

OUR PURPOSE IS the compass that guides our lives. Without it, we wander, reacting to external forces rather than proactively shaping our destiny. Marcus Aurelius believed that understanding our purpose—our reason for waking up each morning—is the cornerstone of self-discipline.

IN *MEDITATIONS*, he reflects: *"I have to go to work—as a human being. What do I have to complain of if I'm going to do what I was born for?"* To him, fulfilling one's purpose was a duty and a privilege.

STORYTELLING INSIGHT:

IMAGINE A WRITER STRUGGLING WITH PROCRASTINATION. She dreams of publishing a novel but spends her days scrolling through social media.

One day, she asks herself, *"What am I here to do?"* Inspired by her purpose, she begins writing for just 30 minutes a day. Over time, those small efforts compound into a completed manuscript. Her purpose becomes the driving force behind her discipline.

ACTIONABLE RULE:

DEFINE YOUR PURPOSE. Ask yourself:

• *What am I passionate about?*
• *What impact do I want to make in the world?*

WRITE it down and revisit it daily. Let it anchor your actions and fuel your discipline.

2. Discipline Over Motivation: Build a Framework for Action

"Turn your desire into stone. Quench your appetites. Keep your mind centered on itself." — Marcus Aurelius

MOTIVATION IS FLEETING—IT comes in waves and often fades when the initial excitement wanes. Discipline, however, is steady and reliable. It's the muscle that keeps you moving forward, even when motivation runs dry.

· · ·

PSYCHOLOGISTS DESCRIBE MOTIVATION AS A SPARK, while discipline is the fuel that sustains the fire. Discipline doesn't rely on how you feel in the moment; it's rooted in habits, consistency, and commitment.

STORYTELLING INSIGHT:

CONSIDER A STUDENT PREPARING FOR EXAMS. At first, she feels motivated to study, but her energy wanes as the days drag on. Instead of giving up, she leans on her study routine—a schedule she set in advance. By showing up daily, she builds momentum and aces her exams, proving that discipline outlasts motivation.

ACTIONABLE RULE:

CREATE a daily routine that aligns with your goals. Break your tasks into manageable steps and commit to showing up, even when you don't like it. Remember, progress is built on consistency, not perfection.

3. Show Up Every Day: Consistency Is Key

"You must build up your life action by action and be content if each one achieves its goal as far as possible, and no one can keep you from this." — Marcus Aurelius

GREATNESS ISN'T ACHIEVED in grand, sporadic gestures but through consistent, deliberate effort. The act of showing up—day after day, regardless of mood or circumstance—is the essence of self-discipline.

. . .

STORYTELLING INSIGHT:

PICTURE A RUNNER TRAINING FOR A MARATHON. Some days, the weather is harsh, and her body feels heavy. But she laces up her shoes and hits the pavement anyway. Over weeks and months, her endurance grows, and she crosses the finish line more potent than ever. Her secret? Showing up, no matter what.

ACTIONABLE RULE:

COMMIT TO SHOWING UP DAILY, whether writing, exercising, or learning a new skill. Set aside time each day for your craft. Celebrate small victories and trust the process.

4. Embrace Voluntary Hardship: Strengthen Your Resilience

"We should discipline ourselves in small things, and from these progress to things of greater value." — Marcus Aurelius

VOLUNTARY HARDSHIP IS the practice of intentionally challenging yourself to build resilience. By stepping out of your comfort zone, you prepare for life's inevitable difficulties. Whether taking a cold shower, fasting, or limiting unnecessary luxuries, these small acts of discipline fortify your mental and emotional strength.

STORYTELLING INSIGHT:

. . .

DURING HIS REIGN, Marcus Aurelius avoided excessive indulgence, even when it was within his power to indulge. He believed simplicity and restraint cultivated strength and focus, traits essential for a leader.

ACTIONABLE RULE:

INCORPORATE SMALL CHALLENGES into your routine. For example, take the stairs instead of the elevator, skip your morning coffee, or wake up 30 minutes earlier. Over time, these practices will build your resilience and self-control.

5. Practice the Dichotomy of Control: Master Your Mind

"You have power over your mind—not outside events. Realize this, and you will find strength." — Marcus Aurelius

THE DICHOTOMY OF CONTROL, a central Stoic principle, teaches us to focus on what we can control—our thoughts, actions, and attitudes—while letting go of what we cannot. This practice reduces stress, fosters clarity, and strengthens discipline.

STORYTELLING INSIGHT:

A YOUNG ENTREPRENEUR loses an essential client due to circumstances beyond her control. Instead of dwelling on the loss, she channels her energy into improving her services and attracting new clients. She rebuilds her business and emerges stronger by focusing on what she can control.

ACTIONABLE RULE:

WHEN FACED WITH ADVERSITY, pause and ask:

• *Is this within my control?*
• *If not, how can I adjust my perspective or response?*

LET GO of what you cannot change and redirect your energy toward what you can.

THE ART of Self-Discipline

SELF-DISCIPLINE IS NOT ABOUT PERFECTION; it's about persistence. It's the daily practice of aligning your actions with your values, even when difficult. As Marcus Aurelius reminds us, *"Choose not to be harmed—and you won't feel harmed."*

BY FINDING YOUR PURPOSE, building habits of consistency, embracing voluntary hardship, and mastering the Dichotomy of Control, you can cultivate the self-discipline needed to navigate life's challenges with grace and resilience.

. . .

As we transition to the next chapter, let these lessons guide you in harnessing your inner strength and staying steadfast on your journey. Remember, self-discipline isn't a destination—it's a lifelong practice that empowers you to become the best version of yourself. Let's explore how to channel this discipline into achieving clarity and focus for a purposeful life. The journey continues.

RULE NUMBER 6: FOCUS ON THE PRESENT MOMENT

*F*ocus On the Present Moment:
Reclaiming Your Now

"With silence comes mindfulness, and thus we become better at choosing our words with kind intent before we express them." — Alaric Hutchinson

THE PRESENT MOMENT is a fleeting gift—a sliver of time in which life unfolds. Yet, how often do we neglect it? We dwell in the past, replaying regrets, or project into the future, consumed by worry. In this oscillation, we lose sight of the only thing we can truly control: the *now*.

THE STOICS, masters of wisdom, deeply understood this truth. They believed focusing on the present moment is the key to cultivating peace, clarity, and intentional action. To them, mindfulness was a meditative practice and a way of life—a discipline of thought, emotion, and action rooted in the here and now.

·   ·   ·

The Challenge of the Present Moment

"Don't be overwhelmed by the panorama of your life. Don't dwell on all the problems that have occurred in the past or may occur in the future. You should ask yourself in every situation of the present: What is there in this work that I cannot bear or support?" — Marcus Aurelius, *Meditations*, 8.36

Imagine a day when your mind races in ten directions at once. You have a looming deadline, an argument replaying in your head, and a to-do list that stretches into infinity. Your thoughts bounce between the past and future, overwhelming and immobilizing you. Does this sound familiar?

Marcus Aurelius faced challenges similar to those we encounter today, even as the emperor of Rome. In his writings, he often reminded himself to concentrate solely on the task at hand. Whether leading armies or navigating political chaos, he found strength by grounding his thoughts in the present moment. For example, during the grueling Marcomannic Wars, Marcus wrote, "What stands in the way becomes the way." By addressing one obstacle at a time, he turned adversity into progress.

The truth is that the past is unchangeable, and the future is uncertain. As Roy T. Bennett aptly said, *"The past is a place of learning, not a place of living."* Returning to the present, we reclaim our power to act, decide, and shape our lives.

The Power of Now

"The future starts today, not tomorrow." — Pope John Paul II

THE PRESENT MOMENT holds unlimited potential. It is the birthplace of every decision, every action, and every transformation.

IMAGINE THIS: You are reading these words. Your mind is here. Your body is here. Your life is happening *now*. Whatever choice you make next—whether to act with courage, kindness, or indifference—shapes not only your immediate reality but the trajectory of your future.

THE STOICS TEACH that we possess only the present moment. Seneca wrote, *"Neither the past nor the future belongs to man; only the present is truly ours."* When we embrace this truth, we gain clarity and focus on living deliberately.

STORYTELLING INSIGHT:

CONSIDER a craftsman sculpting a block of marble. Each chisel stroke is deliberate, focused, and rooted in the present. He cannot undo a mistake from earlier nor predict the final form with certainty. He can only carve one stroke at a time, trusting the process. Like the craftsman, we shape our lives moment by moment.

RECLAIMING THE NOW: A Practice of Mindfulness

"The past has no power over the present moment." — Eckhart Tolle

WHEN WE RUMINATE on the past or worry about the future, we disconnect from ourselves and the present. Overthinking leads to anxiety, paralysis, and a loss of joy. The antidote? Mindfulness.

MINDFULNESS IS the practice of grounding your awareness in the present moment. It is not about suppressing thoughts but observing them without judgment. As Roy T. Bennett wrote, *"Be where you are, stop overthinking, and focus on what you are doing."*

ACTIONABLE STEPS TO **Reclaim the Present:**

1 Pause and Breathe: When you feel overwhelmed, take a deep breath. Inhale for four counts, hold for four and exhale for four. Repeat. This simple act brings your awareness back to the now.

2 Name Your Surroundings: Identify five things you see, four things you feel, three things you hear, two things you smell, and one thing you taste. This exercise centers your senses in the present.

3 Ask Empowering Questions: When consumed by worry, ask:
   o *What can I control right now?*
   o *What action will bring me peace in this moment?*
   o *What is truly important here?*

FOCUSING **on What Matters**

"The future belongs to the competent. It belongs to those who are very good at what they do. It does not belong to the well-meaning." — Brian Tracy

Focusing on the present does not mean neglecting your responsibilities. Instead, it means tackling them one step at a time. The Stoics believed that we can gracefully navigate even the most chaotic situations by addressing what is within our control—here and now.

Storytelling Insight:

A swimmer training for a championship does not think about the end of the race during practice. Instead, she focuses on each stroke, each breath, and each lap. By mastering the present, she builds the strength and skill to excel in the future.

The Wisdom of Tiny Steps

"Step by step walk the thousand-mile road." — Miyamoto Musashi

Big goals can be intimidating, but the moment breaks them into manageable steps. The Stoics encouraged us to approach challenges patiently and persist, trusting that small actions lead to meaningful progress.

Marcus Aurelius advised:

- **Certainty of Judgment:** Ask, *What does this situation objectively require?*

- **Acceptance of Events:** Embrace what is beyond your control.

• **Right Action:** Determine the best course of action and execute it.

ACTIONABLE RULE:

SET a timer for 10 minutes and focus solely on one task. Whether writing an email, cleaning a room, or meditating, give it your full attention. You'll be amazed at what you can accomplish when distractions fade.

QUESTIONING IMPRESSIONS: **The Stoic Virtue of Focus**

"Yesterday is history, tomorrow is a mystery, today is a gift—that's why it's called the present." — Bill Keane

THE STOICS TAUGHT us to question our impressions to cultivate focus. Is this thought helpful or harmful? Is this emotion guiding me or misleading me? By examining your mental landscape, you can align your actions with your highest values: wisdom, courage, justice, and self-discipline.

STORYTELLING INSIGHT:

A YOUNG ARTIST receives a harsh critique of her work. At first, she feels disheartened. However, upon reflection, she realizes the critique offers valuable insights for improvement. By questioning her initial impression, she transforms a moment of doubt into a stepping stone for growth.

. . .

The Gift of the Present

"Knowing is not enough; we must apply. Willing is not enough; we must do."
— Johann Wolfgang von Goethe

THE PRESENT MOMENT is a precious gift—a chance to act, create, and connect. By practicing mindfulness, embracing what is within your control, and taking tiny, deliberate steps, you unlock the power to live fully and intentionally.

AS MARCUS AURELIUS WROTE, *"The happiness of your life depends upon the quality of your thoughts."* You reclaim your thoughts, actions, and life by focusing on the now.

LET this mindfulness practice guide you into the next chapter, where we explore the Stoic principle of finding purpose and meaning in life. With clarity in the present, you'll be ready to discover the path that aligns with your highest self. The journey continues.

EMBRACING STOICISM

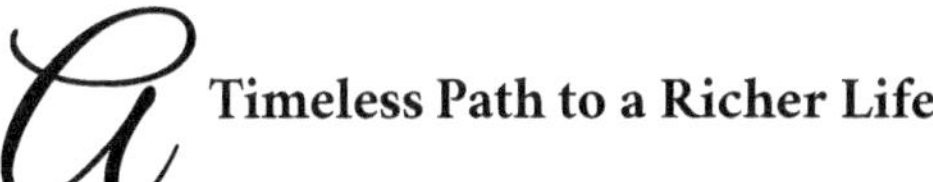 Timeless Path to a Richer Life

"Waste no more time arguing about what a good man should be. Be one." — Marcus Aurelius

STOICISM IS NOT MERELY a relic of ancient philosophy or a collection of abstract teachings for scholars and historians. At its heart, it is an efficient and profoundly human approach to life—an invitation to live intentionally, authentically, and meaningfully. Across the centuries, Stoicism has guided emperors, enslaved people, soldiers, parents, and everyday individuals toward a life of purpose and resilience. As we conclude this exploration, let us reflect on its timeless lessons and how they can transform our lives today.

A PHILOSOPHY for Everyone

"Philosophy is not a luxury for the elite, but a guide for the ordinary."

. . .

THE BEAUTY of Stoicism lies in its accessibility. It doesn't require wealth, privilege, or academic prowess. Instead, it calls to anyone willing to engage with its principles and apply them to their unique circumstances. Whether navigating corporate challenges, managing the chaos of family life, or striving for personal growth, Stoicism offers tools to thrive amidst life's complexities.

STORYTELLING INSIGHT:

IMAGINE EPICTETUS, born into slavery, becoming one of the most revered philosophers in history. His teachings remind us that external circumstances—wealth, status, or misfortune—do not define us. Our ability to control our thoughts, actions, and the meaning we assign to our experiences defines us.

LIVING with Intention and Integrity

"First say to yourself what you would be, and then do what you have to do."
— Epictetus

STOICISM ENCOURAGES us to live purposefully, aligning our actions with our values. It teaches that life is not measured by fleeting pleasures or external accolades but by the depth of our character and the consistency of our principles.

STORYTELLING INSIGHT:

. . .

IMAGINE a farmer tending to his crops. Each day, he rises at dawn, works tirelessly in the fields, and cares for the soil with patience and diligence. He cannot control the rain or the sun, but he can control his effort and dedication. Similarly, Stoicism teaches us to focus on what is within our power—our virtues, decisions, and actions.

EMBRACING Life's Complexity

"You have power over your mind—not outside events. Realize this, and you will find strength." — Marcus Aurelius

LIFE IS a tapestry woven with joy and sorrow, triumph and tragedy. Stoicism doesn't promise an escape from life's challenges; instead, it offers a way to face them with courage and clarity. By accepting that hardship is inevitable, we transform obstacles into opportunities for growth.

STORYTELLING INSIGHT:

DURING A DEVASTATING PLAGUE, Marcus Aurelius continued to lead the Roman Empire with composure and resolve. Instead of succumbing to despair, he focused on what he could control: his decisions, his leadership, and his example. His life teaches us that adversity is not an excuse to falter but a call to rise.

RESILIENCE AND CONTENTMENT from Within

"It is not the man who has too little, but the man who craves more, that is poor." — Seneca

. . .

IN A WORLD OBSESSED with material success and social validation, Stoicism reminds us that true contentment comes from within. Happiness is not found in possessions or recognition but in cultivating gratitude, practicing self-discipline, and nurturing meaningful relationships.

STORYTELLING INSIGHT:

A CRAFTSMAN SPENDS years perfecting his art. He does not seek fame or fortune but takes pride in the quiet excellence of his work. Each piece he creates reflects his dedication and integrity. Stoicism invites us to find similar fulfillment—not in what we gain but in how we live.

A LIFELONG JOURNEY

"Step by step walk the thousand-mile road." — Miyamoto Musashi

EMBRACING STOICISM IS NOT a one-time decision but a lifelong practice. It requires reflection, persistence, and a willingness to adapt. Each challenge we face is an opportunity to apply its principles, deepen our understanding, and grow into our best selves.

STORYTELLING INSIGHT:

SENECA ONCE TOLD HIS STUDENT, "Begin at once to live, and count each day as a separate life." This simple yet profound advice reminds us that every day is a new chapter—a chance to start fresh, learn from our mistakes, and take one step closer to becoming who we aspire to be.

Final Reflections: The Legacy of Stoicism

"The impediment to action advances action. What stands in the way becomes the way." — Marcus Aurelius

As you close this chapter and step into the next phase of your life, remember that Stoicism is more than a philosophy; it is a living legacy. It challenges us to cultivate resilience, embrace adversity, and live with integrity. It empowers us to find meaning in the mundane and purpose in the profound.

Stoicism teaches us to see each obstacle as an opportunity to grow, each hardship as a lesson, and each moment as a gift to cherish. It invites us to live not in fear of what may come but in gratitude for what is.

Actionable Takeaway:

Begin each day with a simple exercise: Reflect on one Stoic principle that resonates with you. How can you apply it to your life today? Whether practicing gratitude, focusing on what you can control, or acting with courage, let it guide your actions and shape your character.

. . .

Stoicism: A Path Worth Walking

"Waste no more time arguing about what a good man should be. Be one."

THE PATH of Stoicism is not an easy one, but it is a rewarding one. It calls us to rise above distractions, embrace life's challenges, and live with purpose and grace. As you move forward, carry its lessons with you:

- **Focus on the present:** Find power in the now.

- **Embrace adversity:** See every challenge as a stepping stone.

- **Live virtuously:** Let your actions reflect your highest self.

MAY Stoicism's wisdom inspire you to conquer each day with a resolute heart, a clear mind, and an unshakable spirit. The journey continues, and the path ahead is yours to shape.

PMA SCIENCE STOIC'S 30 DAILY HABITS

**MA Science Stoic's 30 Daily Habits:
A Path to Resilience and Fulfillment**

"Life is like riding a bicycle. To keep your balance, you must keep moving." —
Albert Einstein

DAILY HABITS SHAPE the essence of who we are. They reflect our intentions, values, and aspirations. When guided by the wisdom of Stoicism and the empowering principles of Positive Mental Attitude (PMA), these habits make life manageable and extraordinary. Let's explore 30 habits to transform your days into stepping stones toward a more prosperous, meaningful life.

1. Gratitude Journaling

"Gratitude is not only the greatest of virtues but the parent of all others." —
Cicero

START YOUR DAY WITH GRATITUDE. Write down three things you're thankful for—your morning coffee, a friend's kindness, or the sunrise. Gratitude shifts your focus from what's missing to what's abundant, cultivating a mindset of positivity and appreciation.

STORYTELLING INSIGHT: Imagine Marcus Aurelius reflecting on the loyalty of his soldiers after a long day of battle. Like him, let gratitude anchor you in life's daily blessings.

2. Morning Meditation

"You have power over your mind—not outside events. Realize this, and you will find strength." — Marcus Aurelius

MEDITATION CALMS the mind and creates space for clarity. Five minutes of mindful breathing in the morning can set a peaceful and focused tone for the day ahead.

PSYCHOLOGICAL INSIGHT: Studies show that meditation reduces cortisol levels, helping you manage stress and improve concentration.

3. Exercise

"It is not because things are difficult that we do not dare; it is because we do not dare that they are difficult." — Seneca

MOVEMENT FUELS both the body and mind. Regular exercise, such as a brisk walk, yoga, or weightlifting, boosts mood, sharpens focus, and builds resilience.

EXAMPLE: Seneca emphasized the importance of physical vitality in living a virtuous life. A healthy body supports a healthy mind.

4. Random Acts of Kindness

"No act of kindness, no matter how small, is ever wasted." — Aesop

BRIGHTEN someone's day with a small act of kindness—a compliment, a helping hand, or a simple smile. Kindness lifts not only others but also your spirit.

PRACTICAL TIP: Seneca believed that humans are social beings meant to support one another. Use every opportunity to be a beacon of compassion.

5. Mindful Eating

"Thou shouldst eat to live; not live to eat." — Socrates

Savor each bite. Focus on the flavors, textures, and nourishment your food provides. Mindful eating improves digestion and fosters gratitude for the meal.

6. Reading for Growth

"The man who does not read has no advantage over the man who cannot read." — Mark Twain

Dedicate time to reading books that challenge and inspire you. Whether it's Marcus Aurelius' *Meditations* or a contemporary self-help book, reading broadens your perspective and nourishes your mind.

7. Daily Affirmations

"Whether you think you can, or you think you can't—you're right." — Henry Ford

Reframe your mindset by repeating positive affirmations, such as "I am resilient" or *"I attract success."* Affirmations rewire your brain to focus on strengths and possibilities.

8. Goal-Setting

"First say to yourself what you would be, and then do what you have to do." — Epictetus

SET ACHIEVABLE GOALS EACH MORNING. Goals provide purpose and a sense of direction, empowering you to tackle the day with clarity.

9. Digital Detox

"All of humanity's problems stem from man's inability to sit quietly in a room alone." — Blaise Pascal

STEP away from screens periodically to reconnect with yourself and the world around you. Even 30 minutes of unplugged time can refresh your mind.

10. Lifelong Learning

"Once you stop learning, you start dying." — Albert Einstein

LEARN a new skill or explore a fascinating subject. Lifelong learning keeps your mind sharp and your curiosity alive.

11. Hydration

"Water is life's matter and matrix, mother and medium. There is no life without water." — Albert Szent-Györgyi

STAY HYDRATED to enhance both physical and mental performance.

Drinking water is the simplest yet most effective way to boost energy and clarity.

12. Visualization

"Imagination is everything. It is the preview of life's coming attractions." — Albert Einstein

VISUALIZE your goals and the steps to achieve them. This mental rehearsal primes your mind for success.

13. Self-Reflection

"An unexamined life is not worth living." — Socrates

REFLECT ON YOUR DAY: What went well? What could be improved? Reflection fosters self-awareness and growth.

14. Connection with Loved Ones

"The bonds that unite us are stronger than the arguments that divide us." — Marcus Aurelius

REACH out to friends and family. A quick message or heartfelt conversation can strengthen relationships and provide emotional support.

. . .

15. Gratitude for Challenges

"The impediment to action advances action. What stands in the way becomes the way." — Marcus Aurelius

VIEW CHALLENGES as opportunities for growth. Gratitude for hardships builds resilience and wisdom.

16. Prioritize Self-Care

"Take care of your body. It's the only place you have to live." — Jim Rohn

ENGAGE IN ACTIVITIES that rejuvenate your mind, body, and soul. Self-care isn't selfish—it's essential.

17. Practice Stoic Principles

"Waste no more time arguing what a good man should be. Be one." — Marcus Aurelius

FOCUS on what you can control, accept the inevitable, and approach life resiliently. Stoicism fosters inner peace and strength.

18. Mindful Breathing

"Feelings come and go like clouds in a windy sky. Conscious breathing is my anchor." — Thich Nhat Hanh

PAUSE AND TAKE deep breaths throughout the day. It's a simple yet powerful way to ground yourself.

19. Avoid Multitasking

"Do everything as if it were the last thing you were doing in your life." — Marcus Aurelius

FOCUS on one task at a time. Multitasking divides attention and reduces efficiency.

20. Set Boundaries

"Daring to set boundaries is about having the courage to love ourselves." — Brené Brown

LEARN to say no and protect your time and energy. Boundaries are a form of self-respect.

21. Cultivate Optimism

"Optimism is the faith that leads to achievement. Nothing can be done without hope and confidence." — Helen Keller

. . .

FOCUS ON THE SILVER LININGS. Optimism fuels creativity and resilience.

22. Practice Forgiveness

"To forgive is to set a prisoner free and discover the prisoner was you." — Lewis B. Smedes

LET GO of grudges and free yourself from the weight of resentment.

23. Acts of Service

"The best way to find yourself is to lose yourself in the service of others." — Mahatma Gandhi

HELPING others not only benefits them but enriches your sense of purpose.

24. Mindful Listening

"Most people do not listen with the intent to understand; they listen with the intent to reply." — Stephen R. Covey

ENGAGE FULLY IN CONVERSATIONS. Mindful listening strengthens relationships.

25. Evening Reflection

"What did you learn today? What did you give today?" — Oprah Winfrey

END your day by reviewing your accomplishments and lessons learned.

26. Positive Self-Talk

"Talk to yourself like you would to someone you love." — Brené Brown

REPLACE self-criticism with kindness and encouragement.

27. Time-Blocking

"The key is in not spending time, but in investing it." — Stephen R. Covey

ORGANIZE your day into dedicated blocks of time for specific tasks. This enhances focus and efficiency.

28. Embrace Discomfort

"Step out of your comfort zone. Comfort is the enemy of growth." — Roy T. Bennett

GROWTH HAPPENS when you challenge yourself. Embrace discomfort as a sign of progress.

29. Appreciate the Moment

"Yesterday is history, tomorrow is a mystery, but today is a gift. That is why it is called the present." — Bill Keane

TAKE time to notice the beauty in the world around you. Awe inspires gratitude and joy.

30. Prioritize Sleep

"Sleep is the golden chain that ties health and our bodies together." — Thomas Dekker

ESTABLISH a consistent sleep routine to rejuvenate your mind and body.

LASTLY,

. . .

Introducing these habits into your daily life is not about perfection but progress. Start small, be consistent, and celebrate your growth. These habits, rooted in Stoicism and a positive mental attitude (PMA), will guide you toward a life of resilience, purpose, and joy. With practice and commitment, these habits will become second nature, transforming your life. Embrace the journey and stay focused on the results. Wishing you all the best on your journey!

As Marcus Aurelius might remind us: *"Each day provides its own gifts."* Open yours with intention.

APPENDIX

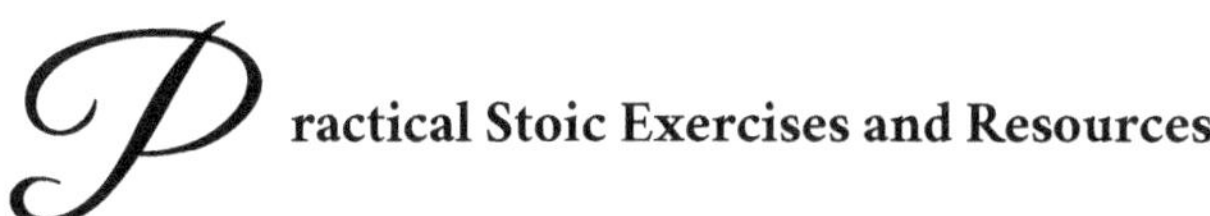
ractical Stoic Exercises and Resources

"Don't explain your philosophy. Embody it." — Epictetus

STOICISM IS A PHILOSOPHY OF ACTION. Its principles, rooted in ancient wisdom, are not meant to remain trapped in theory or confined to pages of books. They are intended to be lived, experienced, and practiced daily. This appendix serves as a toolkit to bridge the gap between philosophy and action, providing exercises and resources to help you apply Stoicism to your everyday life.

STOIC EXERCISES: Daily Practices for Resilience and Clarity

1 MORNING REFLECTION: Begin with Purpose

. . .

"When you arise in the morning, think of what a privilege it is to be alive, to think, to enjoy, to love." — Marcus Aurelius

EACH MORNING, take a moment to set your intentions. Reflect on the Stoic virtues of wisdom, courage, justice, and temperance, and consider how you'll embody them throughout the day. Ask yourself: *What challenges might I face today, and how can I meet them with grace and strength?*

EXAMPLE: Imagine navigating a tense meeting. Respond calmly, listen attentively, and offer solutions rooted in fairness.

2 EVENING REVIEW: End with Growth

"Do not stumble over what is behind you." — Seneca

BEFORE BED, spend a few minutes reviewing your day. Acknowledge your successes and areas where you could improve. Reflect without judgment. Growth stems from honest self-assessment.

PRACTICAL TIP: Ask yourself three questions:

o *What did I do well today?*
o *Where did I fall short?*
o *How will I adjust tomorrow?*

3 CONTEMPLATING the Dichotomy of Control: Focus on What Matters

"You have power over your mind—not outside events. Realize this, and you will find strength." — Marcus Aurelius

REGULARLY REMIND yourself of what you can control (thoughts, actions, and reactions) and what you cannot (others' opinions, external outcomes). You cultivate inner peace and effectiveness by focusing your energy on what you can influence.

EXAMPLE: If a friend cancels plans immediately, recognize their actions are beyond your control. Instead, focus on how you'll maximize your newfound free time.

4 PRACTICING NEGATIVE VISUALIZATION: Appreciate What You Have

"He robs present ills of their power who has perceived their coming beforehand." — Seneca

IMAGINE LOSING SOMETHING YOU VALUE—A job, a relationship, or daily comfort. While this exercise may seem counterintuitive, it deepens gratitude and prepares you for inevitable challenges.

STORYTELLING INSIGHT: Marcus Aurelius, amidst war and political unrest, often visualized losing his empire not to wallow in despair but to remind himself of life's impermanence and the strength he carried within.

. . .

5 Empathy Building: See Through Another's Eyes

"Whenever you are about to find fault with someone, ask yourself the following question: What fault of mine most nearly resembles the one I am about to criticize?" — Marcus Aurelius

ACTIVELY PRACTICE UNDERSTANDING OTHERS' perspectives. Whether in moments of conflict or connection, empathy fosters harmony and enriches relationships.

EXAMPLE: The next time a colleague snaps at you, pause and consider what might fuel their frustration. Respond with kindness rather than defensiveness.

6 Stoic Journaling: Chronicle Your Journey

"Keep your thoughts in order, and they will keep your life in order." — Epictetus

DEDICATE a few minutes daily to jot down your reflections, challenges, and insights. A Stoic journal is a record of your thoughts and a tool for self-discovery and growth.

PRO TIP: Reflect on one Stoic principle each week and how it applies to your life. For instance, write about how practicing courage shaped your actions in a challenging moment.

. . .

Recommended Readings: The Voices of Stoic Wisdom

1 Meditation by Marcus Aurelius

A profound window into the mind of a Stoic emperor, offering timeless lessons on leadership, humility, and resilience.

2 Letters from a Stoic by Seneca

Seneca's letters bring practical advice, from dealing with adversity to finding joy in simplicity.

3 The Daily Stoic by Ryan Holiday and Stephen Hanselman

A modern guide that distills Stoicism into bite-sized daily lessons, perfect for reflection and application.

4 A Guide to the Good Life: The Ancient Art of Stoic Joy by William B. Irvine

This accessible introduction to Stoicism reveals how ancient principles can lead to a more meaningful, contented life.

Online Resources: Connecting with the Modern Stoic Community

Engaging with the modern Stoic community can provide valuable insights and support on your philosophical journey. Here are some online resources to consider:

1 The Stoicism Subreddit: A vibrant online forum where enthusiasts discuss Stoic philosophy, share personal experiences, and offer guidance. It's an excellent platform for beginners and seasoned practitioners to deepen their understanding. https://www.reddit.com/r/Stoicism/?rdt=43939

2 Stoic Week: An annual online event organized by Modern Stoicism that invites participants to "live like a Stoic" for a week. The program provides structured exercises, courses, and community discussions to help integrate Stoic principles into daily life. Stoic Week 2024 is scheduled to start on Monday, October 28. https://modernstoicism.com/stoic-week/

3 The Modern Stoicism Website: A comprehensive resource offering articles, podcasts, and courses on Stoic philosophy. The site is managed by a multidisciplinary team dedicated to applying Stoic principles to modern living. https://colabstaging.co.uk/msbackup/

THESE PLATFORMS OFFER opportunities to connect with others, access educational materials, and participate in events that can enhance your practice of Stoicism.

CONCLUSION: A Living Legacy

"Don't let your reflection on the whole sweep of life crush you. Stick with the situation at hand." — Marcus Aurelius

STOICISM IS NOT a philosophy to be studied from afar but one to be lived. The exercises outlined above are designed to bring wisdom into your daily routine, transforming challenges into opportunities for growth and fostering a life of purpose and peace.

As YOU EMBARK on this journey, remember that Stoicism is not about perfection but progress. Each small step toward practicing these principles is a step toward becoming the best version of yourself.

LET these exercises and resources be your companions, guiding you toward resilience, wisdom, and a deeper appreciation of life's fleeting beauty. And as you navigate the complexities of the modern world, may the words of Marcus Aurelius echo in your mind:

"Waste no more time arguing what a good man should be. Be one."

AFTERWORD

The Enduring Flame of Stoic Wisdom

*"The happiness of your life depends upon the quality of your thoughts." —
Marcus Aurelius*

The Stoics believed that the path to a virtuous and meaningful life
wasn't paved with comfort or guarantees but with discipline, intention, and a profound understanding of what truly matters. Their
timeless teachings were rooted in the idea that while we cannot
control the winds of life, we can control the sails—our thoughts,
actions, and emotions. By cultivating virtues such as wisdom, courage,
justice, and moderation, we can navigate life's inevitable challenges
with dignity and resilience.

As this book, *Stoic Wisdom to Conquer the Day*, reaches its conclusion,
its lessons do not end here. They are not confined to the pages but are
intended to resonate in your daily life—whispering in moments of
doubt, guiding in moments of confusion, and comforting in moments
of struggle. This is a philosophy to read and a way of life to practice,
embrace, and grow with.

A Journey Beyond the Pages

Your journey has no final destination; it is a lifelong endeavor to live fully, with clarity and virtue. Like life, stoicism is not a static practice —it evolves with you. Its principles are universal and deeply personal, shaped by your unique experiences and aspirations.

Picture Marcus Aurelius, writing his *Meditations* not as an emperor preaching to his subjects but as a man grappling with his humanity. Imagine Epictetus, born into slavery, teaching that true freedom comes not from external circumstances but from mastering one's mind. Consider Seneca, who wrote about tranquility and courage while navigating the volatile Roman court. Their struggles were real, their victories hard-won—and their wisdom endures because it speaks to the core of what it means to be human.

Your journey with Stoicism will be equally personal. Maybe you've started journaling to clarify your thoughts, practicing mindfulness to anchor yourself in the present, or embracing discomfort as a path to growth. Perhaps you've begun to notice the subtle shifts—less frustration in traffic, more patience with a difficult colleague, or a newfound ability to pause and reflect before reacting. These are the quiet victories of Stoic practice, which ripple outward to shape a life of purpose and fulfillment.

Stoicism: A Philosophy of Empowerment

Stoicism doesn't promise a life free of hardship. Instead, it offers a framework to face life's inevitable storms with strength and grace. It teaches us to let go of what we cannot control and focus fiercely on what we can—our mindset, choices, and values. This simple yet profound shift is the key to unlocking inner peace.

Psychology affirms what the Stoics taught centuries ago: Our thoughts shape our reality. Cognitive-behavioral therapy (CBT), one of the most effective modern psychological practices, is rooted in Stoic principles. It emphasizes that by changing how we think about a situation, we can change how we feel about it and respond to it. The Stoics were, in many ways, the first cognitive therapists.

Take, for example, the practice of negative visualization, a cornerstone of Stoic thought. By imagining life without the things we cherish—a loved one, a job, our health—we not only prepare ourselves for potential loss but also cultivate a deep gratitude for what we have now. This exercise aligns seamlessly with the Positive Mental Attitude (PMA) approach, which encourages focusing on life's blessings and possibilities rather than limitations.

The Courage to Continue

It is one thing to admire Stoic principles and quite another to live by them. It takes courage to examine your thoughts and actions honestly, to face discomfort and uncertainty without flinching. But the rewards are profound: a life lived with integrity, a mind unshaken by external chaos, and a heart open to joy and connection.

Imagine waking each day with the resolve to embody wisdom, courage, justice, and temperance. Imagine carrying Marcus Aurelius's words in your heart: "When you arise in the morning, think of what a privilege it is to be alive, to think, to enjoy, to love." Imagine facing life's challenges not as burdens but as opportunities to grow, learn, and become.

This is the promise of Stoicism—not an easy life, but a meaningful one.

A Call to Action

As you close this book, I urge you to take Stoicism beyond these pages and into the fabric of your life. Reflect on what resonates most with you. Is it the Stoic practice of journaling? The discipline of focusing only on what you can control? The courage to face adversity with grace? Whatever it is, make it your own.

Explore the rich legacy of Stoic writings. Engage with the modern Stoic community. Practice, stumble, and practice again. Stoicism is not about perfection; it's about progress. It's about showing up daily, doing the work, and becoming better, wiser, and a little stronger.

Gratitude for the Journey

I extend my deepest gratitude to you, the reader. By picking up this book, you've demonstrated a desire to grow, question, and seek. You've joined a lineage of seekers that spans millennia—individuals who dared to ask, "What does it mean to live a good life?"

Your curiosity and commitment breathe life into these words, transforming them from abstract ideas into living wisdom. Together, we've explored a philosophy transcending time and culture, offering guidance for surviving and thriving.

A Final Thought

Let me leave you with the words of Epictetus, a man who rose from slavery to become one of the most outstanding teachers of Stoicism: "No great thing is created suddenly, any more than a bunch of grapes or a fig. If you tell me you desire a fig, I answer there must be time. Let it first blossom, then bear fruit, then ripen."

Your journey is just beginning. Nurture it with patience, dedication, and an open heart. May the principles of Stoicism guide you, inspire you, and empower you to live a life of depth, virtue, and unshakable joy.

With heartfelt appreciation and best wishes for your journey,

Jay Pacheco

129

MARCUS AURELIUS

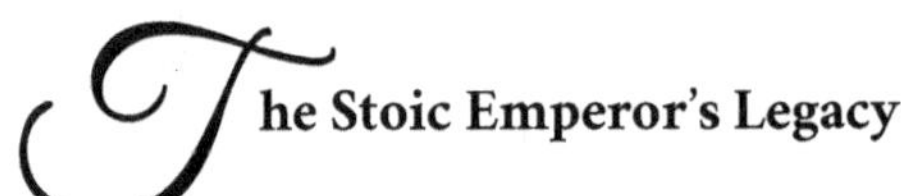

he Stoic Emperor's Legacy

"You have power over your mind—not outside events. Realize this, and you will find strength." — Marcus Aurelius

MARCUS AURELIUS, a Stoic philosopher and Roman Emperor, is a story of wisdom, resilience, and humanity. Few historical figures have embodied the confluence of power and virtue as he did. His life was not merely a tale of triumphs and hardships but an enduring legacy that inspires those seeking wisdom, courage, and balance.

EARLY LIFE: A Philosopher in the Making

BORN ON APRIL 26, 121 AD, in the heart of Rome, Marcus Aurelius was raised in a family of privilege, yet his early life was anything but idle. Imagine a young boy surrounded by towering libraries, his days filled with rigorous learning under the tutelage of some of the greatest minds of his time. His Greek tutors, Aninus Macer, Caninius Celer, and Herodes Atticus, imbued in him a love for philosophy, while his Latin tutor, Fronto, sharpened his intellect.

DURING THESE FORMATIVE YEARS, Marcus encountered the teachings of Epictetus, the formerly enslaved person turned Stoic philosopher. These lessons planted the seeds of his lifelong commitment to reason, discipline, and virtue. Picture Marcus, a boy among scrolls, devouring the works of Plato and Epictetus, preparing not just for a life of privilege but one of purpose.

THE RISE TO POWER: A Stoic's Path to Leadership

MARCUS'S ASCENT TO power was as deliberate as a sculptor shaping marble. His uncle, Antoninus Pius, adopted and groomed him as his successor. When Antoninus passed in 161 AD, Marcus ascended to the throne, a man molded not by ambition but by duty. He stepped into the role of Emperor like an artist on a canvas, ready to paint a life of service and wisdom.

FOR THE FIRST time in Roman history, the empire was ruled by co-emperors Marcus Aurelius and his adoptive brother, Lucius Verus. Imagine them as complementary forces: Marcus, the steady philosopher who embodied reason and virtue, and Lucius, the bold adventurer unafraid of taking risks. Together, they balanced each other's strengths, steering the empire through challenges like the Parthian Wars.

. . .

THE PHILOSOPHER-KING: Insights from a Stoic Emperor

ONE OF MARCUS AURELIUS'S most profound legacies is his writings, compiled into the timeless masterpiece *Meditations*. Picture the Emperor, not on a gilded throne but in the dim light of a campaign tent, pen in hand, reflecting on the nature of life, leadership, and the human condition. His words were not meant for an audience but for himself—a guide to navigating life's chaos.

"The impediment to action advances action. What stands in the way becomes the way." — Marcus Aurelius

FOR MARCUS, life was an unceasing, unpredictable, and ever-changing river. He saw the principles of Stoicism as the steady rock amidst the torrent. His teachings remind us to focus on what is within our control—our thoughts, emotions, and actions—and to let go of the rest. This timeless and universal philosophy is a compass for those seeking clarity in a turbulent world.

THE BATTLEFIELD AND BEYOND: A Leader Among Soldiers

UNDER MARCUS'S REIGN, the Roman Empire faced relentless threats, most notably the Marcomannic Wars. Imagine the Emperor, not cloistered in a distant palace but on the front lines, clad in armor, sharing the hardships of his soldiers. Despite illness and adversity, he led with unwavering resolve, embodying the Stoic ideal of courage in the face of hardship.

. . .

HIS LEADERSHIP WAS NOT MERELY about strategy but about morale. He was a philosopher on the battlefield, inspiring his troops not with promises of glory but with the strength of his example. To him, adversity was not an obstacle but an opportunity to practice resilience and fortitude.

PERSONAL LOSS and Stoic Grace

DESPITE HIS PUBLIC TRIUMPHS, Marcus's personal life was marked by profound tragedy. He endured the loss of many children and his beloved wife, Faustina. Imagine the quiet dignity with which he bore these sorrows, turning to his Stoic principles for solace. He did not rail against fate but accepted it with humility, finding strength in knowing that all is transient.

"Loss is nothing else but change, and change is nature's delight." — Marcus Aurelius

THROUGH HIS PAIN, Marcus taught us that life's trials are not punishments but invitations to grow. His ability to endure heartbreak without losing his humanity is a testament to the power of Stoic philosophy.

A LEGACY THAT TRANSCENDS Time

MARCUS AURELIUS PASSED away in 180 AD, likely succumbing to the Antonine Plague that ravaged the empire. His death marked the end of the Pax Romana, a golden age of relative peace and stability. Yet, his legacy endures—not just in history books but in the hearts of those who seek wisdom in his teachings.

MARCUS AURELIUS WAS MORE than an emperor; he was a guide for humanity. His life reminds us that power and wisdom can coexist and that even the most exalted among us are bound by the same universal truths. He was not a distant figure of perfection but a man who struggled, reflected, and strived—just as we do.

THE ETERNAL FLAME of Stoicism

"The soul becomes dyed with the color of its thoughts." — Marcus Aurelius

MARCUS AURELIUS'S life is a vivid tapestry of philosophy, leadership, and humanity. His writings continue to light the path for those seeking to live with purpose, resilience, and grace. As you navigate the complexities of your own life, may his example inspire you to stand firm in your principles, embrace adversity as a teacher, and find peace in the present moment.

MARCUS AURELIUS'S legacy is not just a chapter in history; it is a living testament to the power of Stoicism. It reminds us that we can cultivate wisdom, courage, and compassion regardless of circumstances. Like Marcus, we can become a rock in the rushing river of life, unshaken and steadfast.

IN MARCUS AURELIUS' words, *"Waste no more time arguing about what a good man should be. Be one."* May we all strive to embody the virtues he lived by, carrying forward the torch of Stoic wisdom for generations to come.

"The wise are not wise because they make no mistakes. They are wise because they correct their mistakes as soon as they recognize them."

— ORSON SCOTT CARD

ABOUT THE AUTHOR

*"Happiness and freedom begin with a clear understanding of one principle:
Some things are within our control, and some things are not."* — Epictetus

Jay Pacheco is a mental health worker, philosopher, PMA and psychology student, and esoteric thinker who advocates for mental well-being. He has dedicated his life to weaving the timeless wisdom of the past into the fabric of modern living. Born in the humble town of San Bartolo Teontepec, Puebla, Mexico, Jay's journey has been self-discovery and global exploration. From the bustling streets of Washington, D.C., to the serene landscapes of Sandefjord, Norway, his life reflects the power of resilience, adaptability, and an unwavering commitment to growth.

In late 2022, Jay founded the **Online PMA Science Platform**, which serves as the platform for **PMA Science University**, still under development. This visionary initiative bridges the wisdom of **Stoicism, Positive Mental Attitude (PMA)**, and **Psychology.** This university and platform represent an academic pursuit as well as a heartfelt mission to empower individuals to transform their lives through a deeper understanding of themselves and the world around them.

A Passion for the Mind and the Human Spirit

For over five years, Jay has immersed himself in studying the intricate workings of the human mind, driven by a fascination with the transformative power of Stoicism, the resilience-building practice of PMA, the insights of modern psychology, and esoteric wisdom. His journey into these fields began as a personal quest to navigate life's challenges and evolved into a profound calling to share these tools with others.

Jay's experiences are not limited to theory or books. He has spent years caring for and observing individuals with unique challenges, including autistic teenagers, adults with diverse disabilities, and those battling dementia. Through these roles, he has witnessed firsthand the resilience of the human spirit as well as his own mind, struggling to convert them into happiness through gratitude, discipline, and tools such as Stoicism, positive mental attitude (PMA), Emotions Revealed (FACS), and modern psychology, along with the potential for growth, even in the face of adversity. His work is a living testament to the Stoic principle: "Adversity introduces a man to himself."

Living What He Teaches

Jay is not only a reader and writer of Stoicism and PMA; he is also a practitioner and an action-taker. In his daily life, he embodies the principles he advocates, consistently striving to cultivate inner peace, wisdom, and a positive outlook, irrespective of external circumstances. He believes that Stoicism, when combined with a PMA mindset and psychological insights, offers a powerful framework for navigating life's complexities and finding joy in even the most challenging situations.

As Marcus Aurelius once wrote, *"The happiness of your life depends upon the quality of your thoughts."* Jay takes this to heart, encouraging others to shift their perspective, focus on what they can control, and embrace the beauty of the present moment.

Inspiration Through Writing

As an author of self-help, children's, psychology, esoteric, and history books, Jay utilizes storytelling as a tool for transformation. His works are infused with lessons that resonate across cultures and generations, providing readers practical wisdom wrapped in engaging narratives. He believes in the power of stories to heal, inspire, and ignite change —a belief that reflects the Stoic emphasis on clarity, simplicity, and purpose.

A Vision for a Better World

Jay's ultimate goal is to inspire others to lead lives filled with resilience, purpose, and fulfillment. Through his writings, platform, PMA Science University, PMA Science Stoic, and personal example, he demonstrates that with the right mindset and tools, it is possible to confront life's challenges with grace and courage.

"Man is not worried by real problems so much as by his imagined anxieties about real problems." — Epictetus

Jay invites his readers to leave the shadows of doubt and fear, embrace the light of self-awareness and growth, and discover the strength within. Whether through Stoic teachings, PMA principles, or psychological insights, his message is clear: life is a journey of growth, and every step, no matter how small, leads us closer to inner peace and joy.

From his humble beginnings in Mexico to his impactful work in Norway, Jay's story reminds us that wisdom knows no borders and that pursuing a meaningful life is a universal endeavor. Through his work, he continues to inspire countless others to see life not as a series of obstacles but as a canvas of opportunities waiting to be painted with the colors of resilience, gratitude, and hope.

"Let us rise up and be thankful, for if we didn't learn a lot today, at least we

learned a little. If we didn't learn a little, at least we didn't get sick, and if we got sick, at least we didn't die; so, let us all be thankful." — Buddha

With this mindset, Jay Pacheco continues to champion the virtues of Stoicism, PMA, and Psychology, guiding others to live lives of authenticity, joy, and purpose.